Kids Before Content

Kids Before Content

An Educator's Guide on Social-Emotional Learning Competencies

Renee G. Carr

ROWMAN & LITTLEFIELD
Lanham • Boulder • New York • London

Published by Rowman & Littlefield
An imprint of The Rowman & Littlefield Publishing Group, Inc.
4501 Forbes Boulevard, Suite 200, Lanham, Maryland 20706
www.rowman.com

86-90 Paul Street, London EC2A 4NE

Copyright © 2023 by Renee G. Carr

All rights reserved. No part of this book may be reproduced in any form or by any electronic or mechanical means, including information storage and retrieval systems, without written permission from the publisher, except by a reviewer who may quote passages in a review.

British Library Cataloguing in Publication Information Available

Library of Congress Cataloging-in-Publication Data

Names: Carr, Renee G., author.
Title: Kids before content : an educator's guide on social-emotional learning competencies / Renee G. Carr.
Description: Lanham, Maryland : Rowman & Littlefield, 2023. | Includes bibliographical references and index.
Identifiers: LCCN 2023004130 (print) | LCCN 2023004131 (ebook) | ISBN 9781475865790 (cloth) | ISBN 9781475865806 (paperback) | ISBN 9781475865813 (ebook)
Subjects: LCSH: Affective education. | Emotions in children.
Classification: LCC LB1072 .C354 2023 (print) | LCC LB1072 (ebook) | DDC 370.15/34--dc23/eng/20230310
LC record available at https://lccn.loc.gov/2023004130
LC ebook record available at https://lccn.loc.gov/2023004131

I dedicate this book to educators. I hope it contains practical knowledge you can use in your schools and classrooms.

Contents

Acknowledgments	ix
Preface	xi
Introduction	1

PART I: NURTURING SELF-AWARENESS FOR EDUCATORS AND STUDENTS — 13

Chapter 1: Strengthening Self-Awareness for Educators — 15

Chapter 2: Strengthening Self-Awareness for Students — 29

PART II: FOSTERING SELF-MANAGEMENT FOR EDUCATORS AND STUDENTS — 39

Chapter 3: Developing Self-Management for Educators — 41

Chapter 4: Developing Self-Management for Students — 49

PART III: ENHANCING RESPONSIBLE DECISION-MAKING FOR EDUCATORS AND STUDENTS — 57

Chapter 5: Strengthening Responsible Decision-Making for Educators — 59

Chapter 6: Strengthening Responsible Decision-Making for Students — 71

PART IV: SUPPORTING RELATIONSHIP SKILLS FOR EDUCATORS AND STUDENTS — 79

Chapter 7: Encouraging Relationship Skills for Educators — 81

Chapter 8: Encouraging Relationship Skills for Students — 89

PART V: ENCOURAGING SOCIAL AWARENESS FOR EDUCATORS AND STUDENTS — 99

Chapter 9: Developing Social Awareness for Educators — 101

Chapter 10: Developing Social Awareness for Students — 105

PART VI: THE DEVELOPMENT OF SEL COMPETENCIES FOR EDUCATORS AND STUDENTS — 111

Chapter 11: SEL Professional Learning Communities — 113

Chapter 12: SEL Implications for School Leaders — 117

Chapter 13: SEL Competencies for Educators and Students — 123

References — 137

Index — 141

About the Author — 149

Acknowledgments

This book was truly a family effort. First, I would like to acknowledge my husband, Zac, who provided insightful feedback and input. I appreciate all the conversations we had about this book and its potential directions. Thank you to my brother Andrew for providing feedback and initial edits for this book. It was important to have a school leader's perspective when writing this book. He was an incredible resource for my first book as well.

Thank you to both my parents for reviewing the book while it was being written. My father provided wonderful content-related feedback and ideas to improve the preface. Thank you to my mother for doing a stenographer-quality proofread. She was able to help me refine the book in the best way possible. I would also like to acknowledge my six-year-old daughter Zoe for always encouraging me and for helping me to think of potential titles for the book, such as "Teacher Ability." That last idea is indicative of what teachers can accomplish when they consider their own well-being in addition to the well-being of their students.

I would like to thank my editor Nimna Uththara Perera, who is a teacher in San Jose, California. It meant so much to have an editor with an educator's eye to review my book. Thank you for all your insights that helped make this book stronger.

Finally, I would like to acknowledge the experiences I have had with my students and fellow educator colleagues. Those relationships and experiences helped frame the message of this book and the need behind it. It was truly devastating for both educators and students to deal with the aftermath of the COVID-19 pandemic. We all acknowledged that we were teaching in some highly unprecedented times due to not only the academic learning loss but, even more importantly, the social-emotional learning loss. We frequently called ourselves first-year teachers. Without the support of fellow educators, it would be even more difficult to get through the school year. This book is for you.

Preface

I have five years of experience as a high school teacher in the mid-Atlantic and I have five additional years of work experience outside of teaching within the field of education.

I wrote and published my first book, *Accountability in the Classroom: Using Social-Emotional Learning to Guide School Improvement*, during the COVID-19 pandemic. I used the content of my dissertation on social-emotional learning (SEL) and my observations as an educator to write that book.

This book is a guide for teachers, students, and administrators to address SEL in the classroom. I first become interested in SEL while working at the College Board, where I was asked by the K–12 policy director to research which states were including SEL in their school accountability systems. When I discovered it was my home state of California, my love for the subject never stopped.

My doctorate is in education, specifically, educational administration and policy studies from the George Washington University. I conducted my field research on SEL in Fresno, California. I am an SEL curriculum trainer for educators all over the country and I have served on the equity and social-emotional learning committees at my school. I made a suggestion for an SEL pilot program at my school last year.

Before becoming a teacher, I worked at American University, the College Board, and on a US Department of Education grant as a government contractor. While working in these diverse roles, I realized that there is not enough guidance for educators to deliver the vital competencies of SEL to themselves and to their students. My hope is that this book will serve as a practical tool that provides research-based evidence for teachers, administrators, and other school staff to use holistically to improve their own learning and practice of SEL.

As a society, we have a lot to gain from helping our children socially and emotionally develop into the best versions of themselves. Educators do not have enough support and time to accomplish everything they hope to achieve for their students. But all educators need and deserve the opportunity to develop socially and emotionally. They must focus on themselves and their well-being before they can help others.

Introduction

Teachers know there are students who need more immediate help than others, and Malachi was one of them. He was always in need of attention, so he would act out in class. It was not until a colleague mentioned how Malachi believed in his teacher's equal, unending love for all her students that the teacher realized she was making a difference.

Just like Malachi, all children need at least one caring adult in their lives. Whether it is a teacher, school staff member, neighbor, family member, or family friend, children need at least one person on their side who caringly holds them accountable.

Human connection matters, and our kids deserve to feel connected to the adults who teach them. Connecting with our students *is* teaching them; it shows them how they, too, can become caring adults later in their own lives.

SEL BACKGROUND

In the modern world, humankind faces many global challenges such as climate change, public health crises, and the increasing disparity between the wealthy and the poor. Students of all backgrounds are going through anxiety, depression, and stress every single day. Many of the jobs these children will have in the future do not yet exist. Among all these social pressures and challenges, students need more from their teachers than just the academic content. Social-emotional learning skills can prepare students to become successful in their careers and in life.

As the educational psychologist Madeline Hunter said, "Kids do not care how much you know until they know how much you care" (Dahlgren and Hyatt 2007). Ultimately, it is vital for the students to see that their educators have a genuine interest in getting to know each and every one of them, which influences them to learn more from their teachers.

The purpose of this work is to help educators understand the use of SEL in the classroom through SEL competencies. This book provides insight into how educators can place their students before content to master emotional intelligence through SEL in the classroom.

This work is written from the perspective of an educator and addresses the ability of both educators and students to effectively apply each SEL competency. The following chapters, which are organized in line with SEL competencies, provide strategies for educators to build these competences. Teachers cannot help their students develop competencies they themselves lack.

The SEL competencies explore five key themes:

- **Self-awareness**: the ability to understand one's own emotions, thoughts, and values, and how they influence behavior
- **Self-management**: the ability to manage one's own emotions, thoughts, and behaviors in a variety of settings while achieving goals
- **Responsible decision-making**: the ability to make caring and constructive choices about behavior and social interactions
- **Relationship skills**: the ability to maintain relationships and to effectively navigate diverse settings, which is foundational to healthy and supportive relationships
- **Social awareness**: the ability to understand a variety of perspectives and empathize with others

Ultimately, SEL provides the ability to develop healthy identities as students gradually learn to manage emotions; achieve goals; empathize with others; build healthy, lasting relationships; and practice effective responsible decision-making.

Featured throughout this book are anecdotes from teachers and administrators who were interviewed for the purpose of understanding their use of SEL in various content areas. These examples provide insight into how one can master emotional intelligence through SEL in the classroom.

A SAFE AND COMPASSIONATE ENVIRONMENT TO LEARN

Students need to learn compassion and kindness not only toward others but also toward themselves. Many school staff members also need to be more compassionate toward themselves, as much as to others. It is more feasible to address SEL with students when the school staff has also addressed SEL skills in themselves.

Educators who cannot regulate themselves will not be able to coach growing children to self-regulate, at least not as effectively. This book outlines ways in which educators can address SEL competencies for themselves *first*, before addressing them for students, and provides guidance for professional learning communities and school leaders.

According to the "5 Dimensions of Teaching and Learning" of the University of Washington's Center for Educational Leadership, students need a safe environment in the classroom to take academic and social risks that maximize learning (University of Washington College of Education, n.d.). To engender this, teachers can implement social-emotional wellness checks and create a safe place to communicate. For example, educators use positive acknowledgement during peer-to-peer interactions to help students more easily connect with one another. "Getting to know you" activities and group collaboration activities are excellent ways to build rapport in the classroom, both between educators and students and among students themselves.

The assumption is that high school students should already have the soft skills necessary for success, which they should have learned in elementary school. This is not always the case because a different level of rigor for SEL is needed in high school than in elementary school. For instance, the perseverance needed to accomplish a task in elementary school is not the same as the perseverance needed to complete a task in high school. This is a detriment to students who need to foster these skills for later life outcomes. Schools are trailing behind in addressing the students' need for SEL at all levels.

Many changes in family structures, economic fluctuations, social trends, and technological trends contribute to socioemotional issues in the lives of children today (Goleman 2005). There is no one better to address these issues outside of home than school-based educators, as they have the most significant contact time with youth outside of the family unit. That said, without effective leadership to implement SEL, inequities among instruction in these skills may initially increase as more schools follow their SEL data metrics and realize the increasing need for SEL.

Successful school reform includes effectiveness, fidelity, and popularity (Cuban 1998). SEL is extremely popular in education media with such outlets as *Education Week*. The perception among the media is that SEL is a valued change, and in terms of Cuban's popularity standard, SEL is crucial.

For a school to undergo a significant change by shifting its culture and climate in the right direction, an effective schoolwide administrational leadership is imperative. The focus is always on lower suspension rates and greater safety on campus—educators want students at school to learn. Ultimately, school leadership is responsible for a positive culture and climate shift, which requires leveraging the talents already present on school teams. Teachers need to be equipped with the tools to bridge the gaps among students' individual SEL needs.

SEL AND EQUITY

In today's ever-changing world, educators cannot possibly expect all students to acquire similar emotional intelligence, as they develop in disparate environments. The opportunities that present themselves to individuals throughout their lives, especially in the United States, are extremely diverse and often inequitable, and the effects of that inequity can be felt decades later.

During enslavement and the period of segregation that followed, generations of Black families were denied equal access to resources and opportunities for success. Black families and other communities of color are playing "catch-up." Therefore, we cannot expect these students to simply develop SEL skills equitably outside schools.

Of all the transition grades (the first year in a new school level), particularly at the high school level, the most challenging is the ninth grade, where students have the most behavioral problems and need the most intervention. They are in a transition grade as it is their first year of high school and they are not accustomed to high school level expectations.

Another issue is that not all students develop a growth mindset to help themselves overcome obstacles. Mindset is a vital component of SEL. People with a fixed mindset see intelligence and skill as static, while people with a growth mindset see intelligence and skills as fluid (Dweck 2006). Without a growth mindset, individuals experience an impediment to overcoming challenges. Schools can attempt to overcome this mindset shift by offering as many resources to the students as possible, including school supplies and clothing.

When planning how they teach SEL skills, especially at the high school level, some teachers automatically jump to the presumption that "the students should know that by now." This is not a realistic expectation of all students. The way in which teachers plan their SEL delivery interwoven with their lessons can contribute to higher academic achievement in students because as teachers use SEL, they address a social-emotional gap within their students to meet challenges. Behavioral choices are shaped by emotions; when students have the skills to emotionally self-regulate, they are better able to navigate complex, rigorous academic content.

Schools can and should provide the necessary professional development throughout the year for teachers to understand and embed SEL throughout the school day. SEL mini-lessons at the beginning of the year set the tone for the rest of the year and should be continuously reviewed while students are praised for their efforts. Although schools can allow their teachers to integrate SEL as they wish, school leaders and instructional coaches can provide them with the tools to implement SEL more effectively.

One such example is the "3 Sign Practice" by the Collaborative for Academic, Social, and Emotional Learning (CASEL). This practice includes a welcoming inclusion, an engaging pedagogy, and an optimistic closure. The welcoming inclusion serves as a method to encourage students to collaborate among themselves to think critically and solve problems. It also serves as a warm-up of sorts, grounding learners in the very nature of being human and communally inquisitive.

Engaging pedagogy motivates students to interact with the content and serves as the main activity of the SEL mini-lesson. Optimistic closures provide reflective opportunities about learning; teachers may provide sentence starters to prompt student reflection and communication. Such sentence starters can include reflections about what students learned, what they enjoyed, what they could teach someone else, or what they look forward to learning in the future.

In our multicultural society, students need a safe, caring, and equitable place to learn where they feel valued and respected. When educators greet their students at the door every day, they are showing interest in getting to know them and are connecting directly with them. The simple act of acknowledging students by name shows that the teacher cares and wants to encourage a positive learning environment. The act of greeting students also reinforces SEL skills, including positive relationship building skills.

SEL AND OTHER SUPPORTS

SEL complements other initiatives in K–12 school systems, such as culturally responsive teaching, trauma informed teaching, Positive Behavior Interventions and Supports (PBIS), and Multi-Tiered Systems of Support (MTSS). All these initiatives place emphasis on creating a school environment in which students feel encouraged, welcomed, and supported; furthermore, they are student centered and data informed. When used together, they can serve all—and especially diverse—student populations and address students' core social-emotional needs.

When initially implementing an SEL curriculum or program in schools, a discussion of the definitions of "culture" and "climate" are extremely useful. In education, we hear these terms used interchangeably, but there is a notable difference in meaning. For instance, according to Hunter (2017), culture describes how group participants behave, repeatedly and habitually. Climate is a product of paying attention to the behaviors and actions in a school and their effects on people.

Our day-to-day behaviors shape the culture of the school. As staff members, we must take the time to foster a strong culture because it is the foundation on which we are able to engage with students. Our culture affects everything we teach, do, and experience. As educators, we must be intentional in our approach. School violence and the COVID-19 pandemic have negative influences on the school climate. When its culture is in place to balance out such negative influences, a school can positively come out a the negative climate crisis instead of adding to the negativity.

THE NEED FOR PROFESSIONAL DEVELOPMENT

Staff training can ameliorate the transition into using SEL. It is not possible to implement SEL techniques successfully without educators believing in—which is distinct from just *knowing*—its benefits. If educators are hesitant because SEL is just one more item on an already-long checklist, they may not teach the SEL lessons as intended and needed.

Leaders must provide professional development opportunities and real examples of successful SEL implementation at schools or in specific classrooms that allow educators to see the growth in students. Data from SEL surveys of teachers and students that demonstrate the positive effects SEL has had on students can be immensely helpful.

Teaching SEL provides an opportunity to master emotional regulation in adults. In whatever we teach, we also become experts, and we must keep in mind that the students are effective teachers in their own way. SEL provides a unique opportunity to close the empathy gap, which has increased drastically since 2001 (Borba 2016).

WHAT'S BEHIND ALL THE ANXIETY IN SCHOOLS?

Students and adults alike are experiencing more anxiety than ever before as a result of societal pressures and the impact of social media. There is a strong desire to prove how happy or fulfilled we are by posting on social media platforms, even if we are not feeling truly happy and fulfilled. This can hurt us because when we do so, we are living in a false reality—and we know it. SEL is an essential way to close the empathy gap, reduce anxiety, and effectively take control over our worlds.

According to Brewer (2021), 67 percent of people's anxiety arises from financial matters. Teaching is not a high-paying profession, which might increase anxiety in educators. Furthermore, 56 percent of people feel anxious about politics. As issues surrounding education have become highly politicized in recent years, teachers may also experience anxiety as a result. Following politics, 48 percent experience anxiety from interpersonal relationships; this is evident in the educational setting by the increased distance between students due to the pandemic.

According to the American Psychological Association (APA), in 2017, 63 percent of Americans claimed that the future is a huge stressor (Brewer 2021). This perception of the future was not uncommon before the pandemic; now, there is even more reason to focus on anxiety reduction for both educators and students.

DIVISION IN SOCIETY

Explaining the source of divisiveness in society, philosophers Jean-Jacques Rousseau and Thomas Hobbes questioned the definition of nature, the role of nature, and whether people are inherently good or bad (Bregman 2019). Hobbes was a pessimist who believed that wickedness is human nature. Rousseau was an optimist who believed all humans are good at heart.

Hobbes viewed people as controlled by fear. He further believed that we must understand our ancestors, especially our primitive ancestors, in order to more fully understand human nature. He theorized that our behaviors are linked to how our ancestors behaved, particularly in survival situations, as illustrated in the book *Lord of the Flies*, in which a group of boys stranded after a plane crash tore each other apart because of their fear (Bregman 2019).

According to Rousseau, people are noble by nature. Rousseau blamed the birth of civilization for our problems. He preferred nature. He thought that we squandered our freedom, finding truth in the maxim, "Give us liberty or all is lost" (Bregman 2019). Rousseau believed in the theory of *tabula rasa*, or the blank slate, which states that all children are innocent and do not have preconceived notions of how society functions. He believed society corrupts children once they learn society's expectations of them.

Based on these beliefs, Rousseau had an interesting take on the role of teachers in education. He communicated a sophisticated attempt to balance the requirements of freedom from the need for control in education. He promoted a delay in the intellectual and moral teachings in early childhood education so that children would learn from their nature first (Iheoma 1997). In particular, he emphasized physical education, which aligned with his love of nature.

Rousseau believed that the role of the teacher was to be wise and to help transform children into adults (Iheoma 1997). According to him, teachers should recognize the wisdom in children, while understanding their ways of seeing, feeling, and reasoning to help them transition into adult forms of these same competencies.

On the other hand, Hobbes focused on self-actualization and transcendence of the individual. He considered people's natural state as a "warre of every man against every man" and individuals' lives as "nasty, brutish, and short". He argued that legal and court systems have the power to ensure that human life is more fulfilling than it was before their creation. Because the role of teachers is to ensure that students understand how to function in society, he did not find child-directed learning to be the right approach.

It is not necessary to side with either Rousseau or Hobbes; however, they elucidate important points about human nature and behavior. Each of us might fall under either philosophy, both, or neither. We do not always follow such strict patterns of behavior. What the two philosophies do is help inform how our perception of truth can hinder or promote individual social-emotional growth.

Anthropologists suggest that in early nomadic societies, children were allowed to play for as long as they pleased. Within these societies, playing and learning were the same. By playing together, children learn to cooperate and navigate social disharmony; furthermore, younger children learn from older children. The culture of play, however, changed significantly once children and their families stayed in one place.

EDUCATION IN HISTORY

The dawn of civilization brought farm labor. It was not until the late nineteenth century, on the heels of the Industrial Revolution, that children once again had time to play. The golden age of unstructured play occurred once child labor was banned and parents left kids to their own devices. In Europe and North America, they roamed free most of the day.

Fast-forwarding to the 1980s, life got busier in the workplace and the classroom. Individualism and the culture of achievement dominated the education and upbringing of children. In the modern era, we are faced with many disruptions and constant changes that are affecting our children. What is the purpose of education? Have we become obsessed with good grades and good salaries? How do we, as a society, define "achievement" and "excellence"? Do the current societal definitions of achievement and excellence necessitate a paradigm shift within societies?

The opposite of play is depression (Bregman 2019). Our modern manner of working without freedom, play, or any intrinsic motivation is fueling an epidemic of depression among children and adults alike. The question should not be whether our kids can handle the freedom; instead, we should ask ourselves whether we have the courage to give it to them. In other words, it is not that our children cannot handle unstructured environments and opportunities; it is that we, the adults, need to look inward and reassess how we teach and interact with our children. What barrier is in the way of adults in trusting children to have vital input into their learning and way of being?

Depending on one's vantage point, society has a shortage of what makes life meaningful—and it is the unstructured play we engage in as children that elucidates one's true sources of joy and interest (Bregman 2019). Children—no, *humans*—learn best when provided with the necessary support and skills; thereafter, we develop autonomy over time if surrounded by a community that brings together people of all ages, abilities, and backgrounds. In return, we are supported by their caring and nurturing peers who are likewise equipped with the necessary knowledge to navigate a socially and emotionally complex world.

SEL FOR ALL

When educators master emotional intelligence for themselves, they can become role models for their students in the acquisition of these skills. Teachers cannot develop SEL competencies in their students if they lack these skills themselves. Compassion and kindness are essential for all. When teachers demonstrate emotional intelligence, it reverberates across departments and the school community. Teachers have a unique opportunity to create a safe place for students to share and discuss ideas. Building a rapport with students and fostering a positive classroom culture are excellent methods to creating a safe place for students.

Most of our society, and high school students in particular, believes that high school students do not need SEL. But these students need SEL as much as, if not more than, other students because they are about to enter the workforce and no longer be a part of the school environment. Building home-school connections at all grade levels improves SEL competencies at school. Educators cannot expect a high level of SEL from all students because just like adults, they are all functioning at different levels.

Segregation, which has historically held back students in marginalized communities, is now at the forefront of discussions about schools. SEL can be a part of the solution to reintegrate schools and create a culture of connection and purpose. Engaging pedagogy opportunities exist for both educator and student reflections. Students must feel valued and respected; this can be improved through culturally responsive teaching, PBIS, and MTSS strategies.

As discussed above, Rousseau's and Hobbes's philosophies describe a dichotomy in human nature and expression. While Rousseau centers on humans as noble by nature, Hobbes suggests that humans are governed by fear, which is responsible for the decisions they make. Teachers play a crucial role in developing people who are whole in both practical Hobbesian ways and idealistic Rousseau methods.

According to Hobbes, teachers should instruct students on ways to become prepared for society. Rousseau recommends that teachers understand the true nature of children as wise and kind, and that they allow children to be themselves before shaping them into what society expects them to be.

In that dichotomy, play is an important aspect of learning for all children because it develops their interests and passions, nurturing the adult selves they will become. The goal of society should be to develop decent people, not just people who will earn good salaries and accolades.

A difference exists between culture (or behavior) and climate (or feeling). Culture affects everything educators do. Staff need training to deliver effective SEL strategies and lessons to their students. They cannot do this work alone; therefore, they need support. Teachers who have not learned how to teach these skills in their teacher preparation programs will feel ill-prepared to deliver on SEL results without adequate training. SEL strategies and programs are essential to assist in the increased anxiety of both students and educators.

REFERENCES

Borba, Michele. 2016. *UnSelfie: Why Empathetic Kids Succeed in Our All-About-Me World*. New York: Touchstone.

Bregman, Rutger. 2019. *Humankind: A Hopeful History*. New York: Little, Brown.

Brewer, Judson. 2021. *Unwinding Anxiety: New Science Shows How to Break the Cycles of Worry and Fear to Heal Your Mind*. New York: Avery.

Cuban, Larry. 1998. "How Schools Change Reforms: Redefining Reform Success and Failure." *Teachers College Record* 99, no. 3 (Spring): 453–77.

Dahlgren, Rick, and Judy Hyatt. 2007. *Time to Teach: Encouragement, Empowerment, and Excellence in Every Classroom with Refocus*. Hayden Lake, ID: Center for Teacher Effectiveness.

Dweck, Carol S. 2006. *Mindset: The New Psychology of Success*. New York: Random House.

Goleman, Daniel. 2005. *Emotional Intelligence*. New York: Bantam.

Hunter, James C. 2017. *The Culture: Creating Excellence with Those You Lead By Growing Leaders and Building Community*. Banbury, UK: JDH Publishing.

Iheoma, Eugene O. 1997. "Rousseau's Views on Teaching." *Journal of Educational Thought* 31, no. 1 (April): 69–81.

University of Washington College of Education. n.d. Center for Educational Leadership. Retrieved from https://k-12leadership.org/resources/?filter=framework.

PART I

Nurturing Self-Awareness for Educators and Students

Chapter 1

Strengthening Self-Awareness for Educators

There is a growing empathy gap that is leaving young people feeling disconnected, lonely, and stressed. Daniel Goleman, the author of *Emotional Intelligence*, describes how poor listening has become endemic. Most teachers are not all right. A CASEL and Yale Center for Emotional Intelligence survey of five thousand teachers during the pandemic found that teachers are feeling anxious, fearful, worried, overwhelmed, and sad. These feelings can negatively impact teachers' mental health and worsen teacher burnout (Martinez Perez 2020).

EDUCATOR WELL-BEING

It is now more important than ever to take educator well-being into consideration. About two hundred thousand teachers leave the profession every year because of challenging work conditions, lack of support, and poor pay (Martinez Perez 2020). When we pay attention to our emotions, we gain new insights that help us make better decisions, leading us to alternative paths we had not thought possible.

Teaching impacts educators' well-being, and sometimes teachers receive little support in learning skills and strategies to improve their own emotional well-being. They often feel drained of energy, with little left for themselves and their families at the end of an arduous workday.

As they pay attention to their own emotions and triggers, teachers can respond to challenging and stressful situations more intentionally and healthily for themselves and for those around them (Martinez Perez 2020). Teaching takes courage because it requires that we face the voices, some internal and some external, that criticize and undermine or block our best work.

When we know how to label our emotions with an expanded vocabulary, we can better communicate our needs with others so we can get the support we need (Brown 2021). Although we have sixty to eighty thousand thoughts a day, we repeat the same types of thoughts every day, every week, and so on (Van Susteren and Colino 2020). As a result, we find it difficult to undo negative thought patterns. On top of that, comparison is a creativity killer. Therefore, we need curiosity and courageous leadership. Curiosity reminds us that we are alive; it is not simply a tool for acquiring knowledge (Brown 2021).

It is time for educators to see themselves as leaders, not only for the sake of their students but also for the adults around them. Many of the same classic leadership techniques work for teachers because they are the leaders of their classrooms. Educators naturally practice leadership every day and at high levels. Teachers and children alike need tools to be able to face failure and disappointment, collaborate, and be adaptable just as much as they need to know academic content.

Daily uncertainties about how educators will be delivering their content has afflicted their sense of confidence. During the pandemic, many educators found themselves unable to rise to the level of innovation required to effectively teach in a remote setting. This diminished their confidence in their teaching abilities, which in turn has had huge impacts on student learning. Similarly, the negative emotions experienced by students dramatically distract them and affect their learning in ways not previously not seen (Martinez Perez 2020). At any given time, a teacher could have several students checked into hospitals for mental health issues.

Teachers help facilitate intellectual development, learning, creativity, resilience, and confidence in their students, all while navigating negative and traumatic experiences triggered by neuroinhibitors indicated by our quick thinking (Martinez Perez 2020). Because of this, teachers have become demotivated and disengaged from everything thrown at them. They are traumatized by their own experiences as well as those of their students.

Educators foster the development of students' academic, social, and emotional abilities. Teachers have an opportunity to nurture caring and supportive relationships that embolden students. The goal of many educators is to help form committed citizens who make the world a better place for all. To this end, fortunately, 90 percent of teachers and school leaders show strong support for focusing on SEL in schools (Martinez Perez 2020).

However, there are persistent systemic inequities. The ways in which we navigate our inner worlds define our everyday thoughts, emotions, and self-stories, and this is the single determinant of our life success (Martinez Perez 2020). We need critical insight into situations through the guidance of our feelings. SEL is a reciprocal process: The social and emotional competences of the adults in the building matter.

Throughout their careers, teachers feel a shift in mindset. Their teaching philosophies change significantly as they dive into their careers. While teachers develop their own perspectives, they are developing their students' perspective as well. Our brains want routine and novelty, and educators crave that for themselves and their instruction.

TEACHER SELF-AWARENESS

Teachers build their own self-awareness from their experiences as educators. They tend to discover more about themselves through the simple act of interacting with students. If they lack self-awareness, they will discover it through their students. Teachers who have students dealing with trauma often experience secondhand trauma; that is, they empathize with the students' stories of neglect, abuse, and hardship. It is difficult to teach something that one does not practice for themselves. Thus, educators can hold each other accountable and be responsible for maintaining a respectful and engaging class by first practicing SEL with each other.

Teachers learn just as much from their students as they do from each other. There is an outstanding need for teacher support and collaboration because of the need to share ideas on handling particular students, parents, and concepts. Teaching students is not geared only toward academic content, but also toward developing them into whole people who can positively relate to one another.

People with a higher emotional intelligence have the ability to self-motivate, persist in the face of obstacles, regulate emotions, keep distress from hindering critical thinking, and empathize with others (Goleman 2005). These abilities are extremely useful in all life situations.

During hardships, students need affirmation from their teachers such as, "There's no reason for you to give up" and "You are more than capable of handling anything." This type of affirmation keeps the learners motivated to work through difficult problems in their projects, assignments, and tests, while building SEL competency at the same time. Teachers can provide encouragement and affirmations along with lessons (Brendtro and du Toit 2005). When they do this, students feel valued and are more likely to perform well in the classroom.

Student reactions of all types and the teacher's own cultural beliefs impact SEL and social teaching practices. Therefore, it is important for teachers to be aware of both how to implement social teaching practices generally and how their emotions and culturally grounded beliefs may impact their social teaching practices (Yoder 2014).

Teachers should explore their emotions. They often go through a full teaching day without noticing or assessing their own feelings. However, once they learn about their own emotionality, they can help their students do the same. When teachers are familiar with the critical role emotions play in learning and interacting with others, they can use this knowledge to design educational experiences that incorporate emotional regulation skills into academic teaching and learning (Martinez Perez 2020).

School staff and students must be inclusive of others, even if it signifies worse outcomes for themselves or the group. Educators and students should be willing to sacrifice performance outcomes for the sake of inclusion and relationship building. When educators place performance above all else, they lose an important component of learning: the social-emotional connection. Students lose the meaning of the content because they do not feel connected to it. Educators can bridge this gap when they help students to understand the content by connecting with them.

USING SEL IN THE CLASSROOM

Creating a comfortable class environment that fosters ease in relationship building with students is an essential goal. One way to improve relationships is to become aware of students' lives. Furthermore, educators can use SEL to teach across all subject areas. Teachers can directly relate to the students and take the time to ensure that the students are familiar with the subject before teaching. Classrooms can be restorative places where students are given the space to engage with teachers on a personal level, even if the students are hesitant to engage in the subject area. From there, the teachers may creatively expose students to the subject matter.

Some SEL-focused educators find it important to have a "homey" classroom to facilitate student comfort. They desire to create a cheerful and relaxing place where students enjoy learning. They do not wish to teach in an industrial or institutionalized classroom, which may demotivate students from learning. They may include couches, easy chairs, home decorations, lamps, photos of family, and hobbies in the classroom. This is not a typical classroom, and students respond positively to the comfort it offers.

The students who enjoy learning tend to thrive more in this type of restorative classrooms; however, if the teacher does not show an interest in getting to know their students or does not express concern for the students, they might feel that the teacher does not care about them. The students may also be indifferent to negative consequences for not doing their work because the teacher may not have clearly communicated these to them. Thus, it is crucial to build real relationships with genuine mutual interest and healthy communication channels, and it is a necessary first step for teachers to build social-emotional well-being in classrooms.

Teachers cannot provide students the social-emotional support they need if teachers themselves are in a poor social-emotional state. Consequently, administrators who are cognizant of the importance of SEL appreciate an upset teacher asking for support in his or her classroom. The result is that there is more social-emotional support for teachers at a school that values this level of administrative support.

Once teachers are confident in their own social-emotional competencies, they can foster improved social-emotional support in their students. They discover better ways to address school needs on a slew of topics, including behavioral issues in transitional grade levels (such as kindergarten, sixth grade, and ninth grade), cultural differences among students from varying backgrounds, and ways to include SEL in the classroom through brain breaks (short, engaging activities given throughout lessons, such as breathing exercises).

SEL fosters positive behaviors in students and improves motivation and peer relationships, which enhance the learning environment for all students. Schools may implement a wide variety of SEL programs to address a range of issues, including conflict resolution and bullying. Teachers benefit from understanding where their students stand socially and emotionally.

SELF-EXPRESSION

There is a price to pay for unexpressed feelings (Rosenberg 2015), so it is essential for all of us to express how we feel. Teachers can model this for their students by expressing their feelings: perhaps sharing when they lose a loved one, when their children are sick, or when they are just having a bad day. This role modeling makes it more acceptable for students to express how they feel. When students are not shown that it is safe to express their feelings, they will bottle up their emotions, and by doing so they are hurting themselves and limiting their ability to connect with others.

Expressing vulnerability can help people resolve conflicts (Rosenberg 2015). When teachers admit that they are uncomfortable or upset about something, they demonstrate that it is permissible to be in that state. Vulnerability does not need to be hidden. Most of us feel this way at various times in our lives, and knowing that their teachers can also feel this way validates students' own emotions.

There is a difference between the way we feel and the way we perceive others' reactions or behavior toward us (Rosenberg 2015). Teachers can help their students build an arsenal of vocabulary around feelings. This vocabulary makes it easier for students to address their emotions and avoid conflicts.

Although used interchangeably at times, there is a difference among feelings and thoughts, and assessments and interpretations (Rosenberg 2015). It is easy to mix these up. Feelings are emotional states, while thoughts are opinions formed in the mind. Assessments can be defined as evaluations or judgments about something or someone, while interpretations are explanations or justifications. Therefore, it is important to be aware of these differences and it is Rousseau-like to promote the expression of feelings for self-discovery because it requires trusting children to understand their own true nature.

To experience better work-life balance, higher job satisfaction, and less burnout, teachers need to minimize unnecessary tasks (Hansen 2018). It is essential for teachers to find ways to teach more effectively without burning out. Instead of collecting every assignment to correct on their own, teachers can have students grade each other or show answers on the board for immediate feedback. They must avoid unnecessarily staying late or taking work home. School systems need to prioritize creating sustainable systems that allow teachers to complete professional responsibilities during the school day through sufficient planning and other creative solutions.

ALTERNATIVE METHODS TO INCREASE MOTIVATION

No day is going to be perfect, which means it is inevitable that teachers need intentional coping strategies. But we need not give up! Instead, we must try again the next time. Teachers need to make sure to not spread themselves too thin. This can include asking for help from administration, colleagues, parents, and students or learning to say no to extras: Do less than obsess (Hansen 2018).

A principal in Clintondale, New York, found his school in the low 5 percent of schools in the middle of the Race to the Top initiative. His school was on the defund list to turn it into a public charter. The principal responded to this situation by flipping the classroom to follow a model he had learned as a football coach to help struggling students. Instead of giving homework, he provided time in class to do the work, and teachers prerecorded lectures and mini-lessons that students could watch from anywhere in their free time (Hansen 2018).

The school had an 80 percent free and reduced lunch student population and had been failing classes and standardized tests. After the classroom was flipped, the students were succeeding again and teachers were taking less work home (Hansen 2018). The moral of the story is that educators can change the way the work is done to best serve both the teachers and the students—SEL is for all stakeholders.

The redesign mentioned by Dan Pink is to drive "functional fixedness," or our inability to problem solve due to our fixation on how work has always been done. One way to avoid this is to ask "stupid questions" and rethink conventional classrooms. A classroom does not have to be a place where teachers lecture; it can be a place where coaches help struggling students (Hansen 2018).

Changes can start small first and then be scaled up. The Clintondale principal started with one classroom and gradually expanded his method to the whole school. Smarter grit is preservative, and it is key to listen to the needs of those you want to influence. Evidently, there are issues with under- and overcollaboration. It is difficult to find the right equilibrium here, so providing feedback to administration and using whatever flexibility you have is essential for success (Hansen 2018).

SELF-COMPASSION

The development of self-compassion is important in our communication to ourselves and with others. Educators must evaluate themselves in ways that promote growth rather than self-hatred when a lesson does not go well or when a student is being particularly difficult. Instead of interpreting challenging events in ways that will hurt educators, such events should be interpreted as learning opportunities, and educators must be ensured that ongoing decisions serve them.

Too often, teachers judge themselves for mistakes when instead they can benefit from the mistakes and take them as learning opportunities. Errors are ways we can see limitations and guide ourselves through growth. Change needs to be motivated by a clear desire to enrich teaching without unwanted feelings of shame and guilt, which are forms of self-hatred (Rosenberg 2015). Educators should try to avoid telling themselves what they should have done to make something better. This type of behavior implies that there was no choice with the action.

Judgmental self-talk deters possibilities in the classroom. Inner judgment, shame, and commands of oneself prevent innovation, continued growth, and the overall improvement of teaching. Teachers who are stifled by their inner critic can no longer perform the duties of their role, which is already a demanding one.

According to Neff (2011), there are three components to self-compassion—self-kindness, common humanity, and mindfulness. Self-kindness is understanding the inner critic, common humanity is recognizing a connection with others rather than feeling isolated, and mindfulness is holding a balanced awareness rather than ignoring pain. All three of these components must be infused to truly enjoy the benefits of being self-compassionate.

Mindfulness consists of being focused on the present and practicing acceptance. Being focused on the present means staying engaged in the current activity and not being distracted by anything else. Acceptance is the ability to open to your experience as it occurs (Gillihan 2018). It also means letting go of preferences. It does not help to hold on too tightly to expectations; it is more beneficial to loosely hold them but not be overly attached to them. Having expectations for outcomes that may not occur can only hurt us. Students can benefit greatly from this knowledge.

Unfortunately, Western society instills in us the value of being kind to everyone but ourselves. Teachers are already blamed by society for the troubles in education. The last thing they should do is to blame themselves. Teachers need self-compassion to avoid the continued downward slope of perceived failure. Self-kindness brings the ability to soothe and calm troubled minds. It allows everyone to see themselves as worthy human beings who deserve care (Neff 2011). Once insecurity is out of the way, teachers can pursue their goals and achieve them with increased confidence.

Self-compassion is knowing that, through trial and error, it does get easier with time. It is important to recognize your self-critic right away and to ask him or her to calm down while you figure everything out. This is where self-reflections play a critical role in teacher growth. When teachers write down what did not go well during a lesson, they are less likely to repeat the same mistakes when teaching the same lesson or other lessons in the future.

An important component of self-compassion is the ability to sympathize with the part of oneself that initially made the mistake and the part that regrets the action. There is a process in mourning and self-forgiveness that can be liberating for learning and growing.

IMPROVING COMMUNICATION

In his book *Nonviolent Communication*, Rosenberg (2015) suggests four steps, in the form of questions, to express empathy; teachers can use these for themselves in the classroom. Incorporating these steps in their lesson delivery will increase not only their own self-awareness, but also that of their students. The following questions have been slightly adjusted for educators.

These questions can also be taught to students to help them increase their own self-awareness.

1. What am I observing?
2. What am I feeling?
3. What am I needing right now?
4. Do I have a request from myself or from a student?

When we ask these questions of ourselves, we can take a break from any difficult situation and listen deeply to our own needs. Emotions teach us what works and does not work well for us. They teach us how to decipher what matters the most.

As teachers instruct their students on how to share their feelings, it is equally important to note that their thoughts and interpretations should not always be shared. It is the way in which their thoughts, assessments, and interpretations have shaped their feelings that should be addressed. Teachers should regularly model empathetic behaviors so their students can do the same.

Traditionally, preservice teacher programs did not require teachers to self-reflect. But that is changing. Teachers' self-awareness regarding how they communicate their lessons to the students is recognized as a valuable resource for effective classrooms. When teachers are self-aware of their own tendencies, they are also more cognizant of their students' self-awareness. This knowledge enhances their ability to effectively interact with their students, which will also positively impact the teachers' lives outside of the classroom (Marzano 2017).

A critical part of being self-aware educators is recognizing vulnerability in ourselves and in our students. Author Brené Brown suggests cultivating the need for accepting shame, learning from mistakes, and improving upon oneself. These lessons are especially important for educators to take to heart. In her book *Rising Strong: How the Ability to Reset Transforms the Way We Live, Love, Parent and Lead*, Brown (2015) presents several tools to cope with the stressors of shame, feeling like an imposter, and even grief, which can transform us into leaders.

SELF-EVALUATION

The ability to recognize our own shortcomings makes us more likely to rise above them. As Brown (2015) suggests, we are not perfect, and accepting that truth early on will better prepare us for the future. As we share our feelings of vulnerability with our students, they can better understand that even though it is normal to feel "not good enough," it does not mean that we need to stay there. We can recognize the feelings and move on; we are not required to let our feelings control our decisions. The process of recognizing these emotions liberates both educators and students to gain complete self-actualization.

Emotional wake is the emotions one feels after someone in authority, such as a teacher, has left (Scott 2002). Teachers can either soothe their students or cause panic attacks. Educators cannot lead in the classroom if they are unconscious of what their students are feeling. It is easy to ignore comments or feedback, but there is a toll for being unconscious of others' feelings. Even a simple comment can cause resentment and misunderstanding.

Fierce conversations are needed to avoid the emotional wake (Scott 2002). As educators, we must always have check-in conversations with our students to help them better understand the direction of the curriculum and to make sure that they are emotionally all right.

Educators should take responsibility for their emotional wake because our emotional wake determines the story that is told about each of us. It is best to deliver your message without emotional baggage (Scott 2002). What is your story? How would you like to be perceived? What is the legacy you would like to have? If your students could tell one story about you, what would it be? What is your ongoing conversation with your students? When educators keep these questions in mind, they are better able to hold themselves accountable to the possible emotional wake or damage they could inadvertently cause their students.

A motivational speech is for the purpose of where we are going. Why are we going there? How are we going to get there? Who is going with us? What is the spirit? What are the values? Educators can conduct a motivational speech posing these questions when students are confused about the direction. Change the world one lesson and one conversation at a time (Scott 2002). No single lesson is guaranteed to change the outcome of a class, but it can; keep this in mind when doing motivational lessons.

Being an authentic and passionate educator is not easy—in fact, it is quite tiresome—but it is the best way to serve oneself and one's students. Many educators work best with creative freedom, collaboration with colleagues, and the resources that encourage them to improve their craft every day. There is grace that comes with ongoing personal transformation. Educators can also deliver lessons with affection while emotionally connecting with their students. To achieve this, teachers need ongoing support, whether that comes from within the building or outside of it.

The ability to connect with students on a human level is irreplicable. That is why it was so difficult to teach online during the pandemic. Changing the way in which we talk to ourselves ultimately changes the way we interact with students.

There needs to be more appreciation and praise for the work that students do. Messages to guardians help when students do well in general and on projects, presentations, and tests. Just like educators need praise, students do, too. There is not enough of this for either educators or students, but educators can change that.

TAKEAWAYS FOR EDUCATOR SELF-AWARENESS

Truth is multifaceted because experiences and perceptions are unique to each person. When your emotions are negative, you are going to increase the negative emotional wake. If you allow space for interpretation when you are emotionally triggered by a student, you will become a crucible for a strong, resilient vessel in which significant change and transformation can occur.

There is an empathy gap in schools, and teachers are not all right. Teacher well-being and burnout have become even bigger concerns than they were prior to the pandemic. Educators must pay attention to their emotions and eliminate negative thoughts to improve their collective well-being. Educators should recognize that they are leaders. They can empower themselves by believing they are leaders and describing themselves as leaders to others. After everything educators have endured, they should feel empowered by their ability to innovate and deal with daily uncertainties and trauma.

Educators recognize the need for SEL in schools and its potential to help our children. A shift in the current mindset is underway. Teachers need to collaborate with other educators and share the tools to self-regulate. Teachers often do not take the time to notice how they feel throughout the day. But unfortunately, there is a price to pay for unexpressed feelings. This needs to be addressed, and it can be changed by incorporating emotions into teaching and learning. SEL can be used in all content areas as we become more aware of students' lives. Such restorative classrooms help students learn better.

Teachers can successfully manage their large workloads by minimizing unnecessary tasks and by not taking work home. They can increasingly become self-compassionate and eliminate regrets by avoiding perceived failure. Emotions teach us about ourselves, and they are there for us to learn. Teachers are already being blamed for enough; they do not need to blame themselves as well. On that note, self-reflection can be a very useful tool to help improve instruction and self-regulation.

QUESTIONS FOR REFLECTION

1. How can teachers integrate mindfulness into their lives?

2. How can teachers be more self-compassionate and self-kind?
3. How can teachers eliminate harmful self-talk regarding their work?

ANSWERS TO QUESTIONS FOR REFLECTION

Educators can integrate mindfulness into their lives through meditation and by carefully considering their choices. They can further seek motivation for introspection and mindfulness by considering other cultures and perspectives. Mindfulness is the awareness that arises through intentionally and nonjudgmentally paying attention in the present moment. (Brewer 2021).

Educators can be more self-compassionate and self-kind through setting boundaries that facilitate more of a work-life balance. They should forgive themselves for what they cannot control. Educators can eliminate harmful self-talk regarding their work by having accountability partners and learning to forgive themselves. They can consult mentors who will assure them that they are not alone in making mistakes. Furthermore, they reflect upon lessons that go poorly and use the growth mindset to deliver better lessons in the future.

REFERENCES

Brendtro, Larry, and Lesley du Toit. 2005. *Response Ability Pathways: Restoring Bonds of Respect*. Cape Town, South Africa: Pretext.

Brewer, Judson. 2021. *Unwinding Anxiety: New Science Shows How to Break the Cycles of Worry and Fear to Heal Your Mind*. New York: Avery.

Brown, Brené. 2015. *Rising Strong*. New York: Penguin Random House.

Brown, Brené. 2021. *Atlas of the Heart: Mapping Meaningful Connection and the Language of Human Experience*. New York: Random House.

Gillihan, Scott. 2018. *Cognitive Behavioral Therapy Made Simple: 10 Strategies for Managing Anxiety, Depression, Anger, Panic, and Worry*. Emeryville, CA: Althea Press.

Goleman, Daniel. 2005. *Emotional Intelligence*. New York: Bantam.

Hansen, Morten T. 2018. *Great at Work: How Top Performers Do Less, Work Better, and Achieve More*. New York: Simon and Schuster.

Martinez Perez, Lorea. 2020. *Teaching with the Heart in Mind: A Complete Educator's Guide to Social Emotional Learning*. New York: Brisca Publishing.

Marzano, Robert J. 2017. *The New Art and Science of Teaching*. Bloomington, IN: Solution Tree.

Neff, Kristin. 2011. *Self-Compassion: The Proven Power of Being Kind to Yourself*. New York: HarperCollins.

Rosenberg, Marshall B. 2015. *Nonviolent Communication: A Language of Life*. Encinitas, CA: PuddleDancer Press.

Scott, Susan. 2002. *Fierce Conversations: Achieving Success at Work and in Life, One Conversation at a Time*. New York: Viking.

Van Susteren, Lisa, and Stacey Colino. 2020. *Emotional Inflammation: Discover Your Triggers and Reclaim Your Equilibrium during Anxious Times*. Louisville, CO: Sounds True.

Yoder, Nicholas. 2014. *Self-Assessing Social and Emotional Instruction and Competencies: A Tool for Teachers*. Washington, DC: American Institutes for Research. Retrieved from https://files.eric.ed.gov/fulltext/ED553369.pdf.

Chapter 2

Strengthening Self-Awareness for Students

Mindfulness may come naturally to some students and not to others. Some students are naturally able to self-soothe and calm themselves, while others are full of energy, unable to stay still and quiet. It is important to keep in mind that students will turn to mindfulness in their own time, when they are ready. Children and teenagers cannot be pushed beyond their comfort levels. Adults should not force students to speak about uncomfortable feelings or to meditate. The first step in creating a mindful practice is to acknowledge the reason for doing so (Greenland 2010).

COMMUNICATING SELF-AWARENESS FOR STUDENTS

Greenland (2010) suggests three questions to ask children about what they think and what they communicate to others: Is it true? Is it necessary? Is it kind? These three questions can be placed on a poster in the classroom to discuss a multitude of issues affecting children today, such as cyberbullying.

Unfortunately, the sort of bullying behavior where students criticize their peers is exactly what Hobbes meant when he described human life as nasty, brutish, and short. When adults encourage children to think about how their statements can negatively impact their peers, they are less likely to hurt others. This is an important life skill that will instill kindness in students that will positively impact their behaviors in the future. At first, they may question why these questions are being taught; however, when their teachers explain the purpose behind them, children are more likely to use them.

Mindfulness and reflection journaling can help learners dispel any negativity they have around learning and the subject matter. Siegel and Payne Bryson (2012) propose a wheel of awareness to better understand our own self-awareness in improving mindfulness. He suggests that the mind can be depicted as a bicycle wheel where the mind is the hub. The rim symbolizes anything we can pay attention to or be aware of, such as our thoughts and feelings, our dreams and desires, our memories, our perceptions of the outside world, and the sensations from the body. The hub is where we become aware of everything and pay attention to in terms of sensations etc. This is where we make our decisions, and it is the part of the brain where we connect with others. Our awareness comes from the hub as well.

The wheel of awareness can be used to show that students do not need to stay focused on just one part of the wheel when in distress. There are many other components of the wheel worth considering. This is a pertinent tool

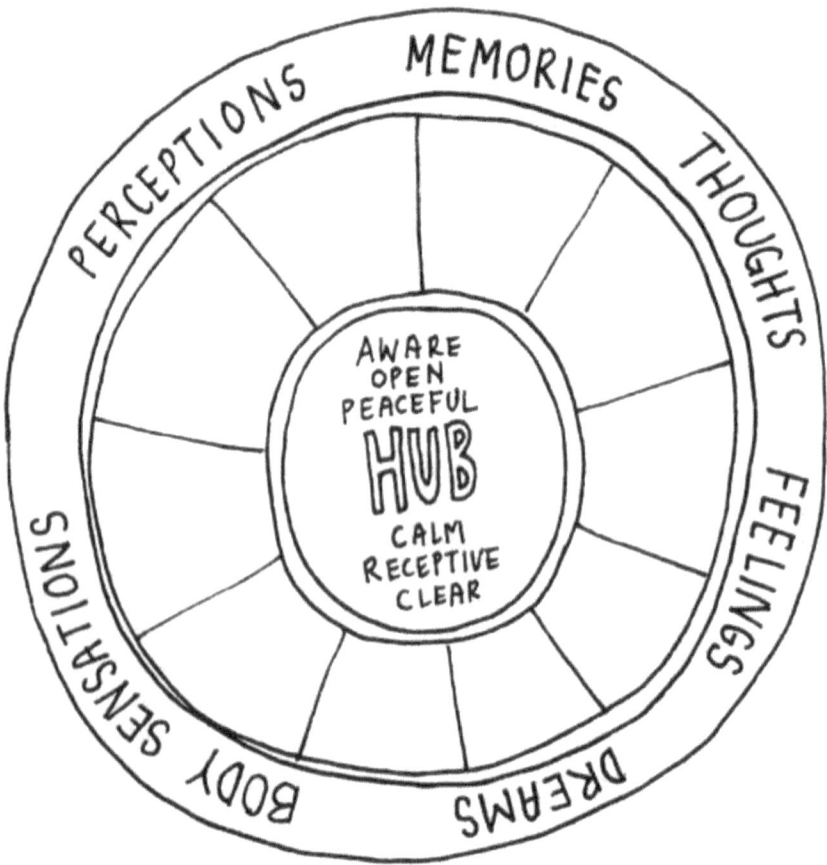

Figure 2.1. Wheel of Awareness. Source: Siegel. (2012). *The Whole-Brain Child.* New York: Random House.

to use for students to learn that they do not need to become hostage to a negative feeling. With practice, students can learn to redirect their attention in ways that are more helpful for themselves, particularly during challenging moments.

When students become aware of the multitude of emotions they are experiencing, they can begin to acknowledge them and perhaps even embrace them as parts of themselves. They do not need to let these define who they are. Instead, they can use the wheel of awareness to refocus on other rims of the wheel. Students no longer need to be victims of their emotions and forces beyond their control (Siegel and Payne Bryson 2012). They can become active participants in the process of deciding and affecting how they think and feel.

When students are stuck on one part of the wheel and cannot return to the hub, educators can help them by discussing the wheel of awareness and their ability to understand their own feelings. It helps them to understand that feelings arise and fall away, and that they do not need to control them. On average, an emotion stays for about ninety seconds and then dissipates (Siegel and Payne Bryson 2012). Sharing that knowledge with students is powerful. When they recognize this, they can enjoy life and make decisions from their hub. Students can even create their own wheel of awareness to express what is important to them.

The wheel of awareness and similar tools can be used to address SEL needs in underserved populations. It is especially important that schools develop SEL competencies in students whose families have immigration issues, drug-related issues, and homelessness. These students may not know how to cope with these issues socially, emotionally, or academically; SEL provides an answer to the myriad dilemmas faced by these students in their everyday life.

STUDENT TRAUMAS AND SELF-AWARENESS

When students are poor and live out of their cars and hotels with extended family and friends, they need methods to alleviate the stressors they encounter daily. Meanwhile, students who live in stable homes with married parents face other types of stressors, including pressure to excel, participate in clubs and sports, and attend college. Students who live in group homes, go to jail, belong to gangs, or use, abuse, or sell drugs have different kinds of issues. Educators know that no child chooses the life they are in; they are born into it.

The only solution that provides hope and effective tools to all these students is SEL. All students are dealing with traumas, and traumas yield profound social-emotional needs. The school leadership must believe that

SEL can address misbehaviors, particularly for ninth graders. Without SEL, schools with diverse social-emotional needs could possibly present a hostile learning environment. Thus, the administrative goal should be to provide students who have fewer resources with the opportunities to self-regulate their emotions to succeed in their academic and social lives.

TARGETING TRANSITION YEARS

The positive actions of administrators make a tremendous impact on the school climate and culture. Especially, administrations coming from middle schools to high schools understand the need to address ninth grade misbehaviors and they turn to SEL as the solution. Ninth graders, who are experiencing a transition year between middle school and high school, do not always have the self-awareness required for the high school environment. Consequently, the ninth grade is where most behavioral issues occur. SEL instruction must be tailored to these students.

Many school districts already mandate a Positive Behavior Interventions and Supports program that makes the implementation and adaptation of SEL approachable for the school. This early access to PBIS may lead a school to a state where SEL thrives and continues to be at the forefront of discussion.

Ninth graders may not have a clear sense of where they want to go and what they want to do. At this transition stage, they find themselves held to a higher standard. Often they find themselves in a large school setting for the first time. Some need to learn skills such as social awareness, because ninth graders are often the ones to get in trouble, get suspended, and go in and out of class. When they are upset, many ninth graders do not understand how to approach others in a way that will not escalate the situation by causing a fight or altercation.

Behavioral issues with the ninth graders can arise because younger students are not held accountable when they graduate from one grade to another. Students in kindergarten through eighth grade can keep advancing to the next grade even if they fail, but when they get to high school, they must earn credits to be promoted to the next grade.

Students whose reading ability is below their grade level struggle; for instance, they may have difficulty understanding their daily tasks. Many students in the ninth grade go through the same struggle because they will be behind on credits. This is not the case in all school districts but is often an issue where in districts facing a lack of resources.

In school systems that promote SEL at all levels, there will be fewer behavioral issues in the ninth grade. Students who have fewer problems socially and emotionally show less problematic behavior. They are better able to manage their emotions when there are strong adult relationships in place at school and/or at home.

SEL AT SCHOOL

Even within the same school district, schools incorporate SEL into their curriculum in different ways. If all the schools completed the same work on SEL as do with their regular curriculum, the students would improve their understanding of the importance of regular school attendance and consequences of misbehavior. However, consequences of misbehavior vary drastically from one school to another; while one school may suspend a student for a misbehavior, another may simply call home.

Other consequences include in-school suspension and mediation. Because every student is different, there can never be a one-size-fits-all approach to mitigating misbehaviors and assigning uniform consequences for transgressions. Just as there is a need for consistent academic mastery expectations across the district, the district also must focus efforts on consistency with SEL across all schools. The lack of consistency is detrimental for students who need both the academic and socioemotional preparation for high school, where expectations are higher.

The needs of each student are unique. However, not all teachers realize that they need to use SEL in the classroom. The administration's goal for teachers should not be limited to just students focusing on academic content and skills; it must include teachers incorporating the SEL competencies in student learning.

Administrators should seek out advice from students to determine what the school's needs are and how to best address those needs. They may also hold brainstorming sessions during staff meetings to discuss the needs of the students are and how they can best be met.

Teachers should think about what skills they need to use to reach their students within the content area. These ultimate goals specifically include planning and incorporating SEL skills along with academic content. How are we teaching, or how can we use SEL as a tool to help students learn SEL skills? Schools can offer teacher workshops to help educators build SEL teaching capabilities; for instance, one session may focus on how to increase the growth mindset in students, which is a foundational element of SEL.

Teachers must be provided with the necessary guidance and training if SEL is to have an impact on improving student behavior and academic performance. Administrators in schools that use SEL programs often express their satisfaction with the programs. But there is never going to be one program that fits all school populations. Schools can make the most of the program they use, and it is up to the school to use a variety of resources and perspectives presented by the SEL program.

The type of SEL program adopted by a school may not help administrators map out how the school can improve. It is a combination of feedback from staff, students, and the community that can best promote schoolwide improvements through SEL. A school can reach its peak success when the program, actors, and delivery work together.

Educators strive to ensure that their students learn to analyze situations and make the right decision. For example, the students in an English language arts (ELA) class can become comfortable asking themselves, "Can I relate this to what Okonkwo endured in *Things Fall Apart*?" Reading passages of literary fiction, in comparison to nonfiction or popular fiction, enhances the empathy of the reader. ELA teachers develop the ability for students to relate to characters, and ELA classes read such novels because teachers want their students to better empathize with others and to understand their motivations, their flaws, and why they make the decisions that they do. Those are the skills that they are trying to enforce: They want to ensure that their students learn how to analyze situations and discern the right decisions to make.

Educator goals have shifted over the years, and now teachers nurture students to find their own unique voices. Teachers may help their students express and define their voices on their own terms, in the way that they construct them, choose them, and use them. This process and the results have great power as well as an enduring impact on any individual; in fact, this is the reason why some decide to teach.

Educators wish to equip their students with the skills to navigate that world. When teachers can speak effectively, write effectively, and read something life altering, they gain new ideas that shift their mindset, which they can then relate to their students. These experiences provide a new perspective on the world.

Metaphorically, an SEL-focused teaching philosophy is to give their students the key to unlock their own voices and power because the students are not aware of the existence of their voices. SEL teaching helps students understand their own power by providing them models through the opportunity to apply their voices and choices when writing. Teachers hope this improves their students' self-awareness and helps them learn to find, express, and develop their own unique voices.

Classrooms can be filled with resources that identify skills and explain the importance of SEL in their everyday lives, without students realizing it. These subtle reminders are intended to be ingrained within students' behavior over time, as other classes also relate to the same crucial life topics.

One example of this is a poster in a writing course that says, "Family, Freedom, Livelihood, and Opportunity." Another example is a poster on

Hamlet that lists relationships, revenge, sanity and madness, philosophy, lies, and deceit as themes. The class rules can be simple and easy to remember—be respectful, be responsible, and be reasonable—or they can be class-created contracts where the rules are decided by the class at the beginning of the year under the facilitation of the teacher.

Campus security staff can provide time-outs, pep talks, and self-awareness conversations, and they can discuss what the students could have done differently in a particular situation. This effort places the responsibility on students to contemplate which actions they might change in the future.

A variety of subject area teachers can incorporate SEL practices through such means as decorating classrooms, making subjects more tangible by using real-world examples, and providing stress relief to students through breathing breaks. This variety in SEL practices is a result of the differences among educators in subject area and teaching philosophy. These variations allow students to experience a way to socioemotionally develop in the manner best suited for them.

Many ELA classes already practice SEL at a high level. Aligning with a health-focused curriculum in an ELA class, the topic of a lesson can be mindfulness and meditation; the SEL skill focus of this lesson can be self-awareness. For instance, students can annotate an article about the scientifically proven benefits of mindfulness and meditation. Such an article may discuss yoga, body awareness, daily homework, eating, and household chores as instances where one can focus on being in the moment instead of thinking about stressors. The message is to pay full attention to what one is doing at the time.

Teachers can use SEL during a brain break activity where students could calm down, escape, and focus. A new trend is to have a five-minute walking pass that discusses how to relieve stress through breathing deeply and letting the mind unwind. Students can also take a break to listen to the soothing sounds of a piano while watching a collection of the planet's most beautiful scenery.

One idea is allow students to access this type of brain break by scanning a QR code that directs them to a YouTube video. A brain break box may contain stress relief balls, a foam cake, and small toys students can play with while they reorient their minds. Having signs with affirmations such as "We believe in you" and plants at every station creates a homelike environment at school.

TAKEAWAYS FOR STUDENT SELF-AWARENESS

Students need opportunities to collaborate, problem solve, and connect with their peers. When teachers use activities to facilitate these opportunities, they are providing a foundation of skills for the lifelong learning and success of the students. One important way to do this is to ask open-ended questions and provide a silent thinking time to students at all levels. Elementary students can do morning circles and name games. To conclude lessons at the elementary level, closing circles are an excellent way to reconnect with students and reflect upon the day's learning while also discussing the next day's lessons and what the students are looking forward to learning.

Mindfulness can come naturally for some but not for others. To avoid hurting others emotionally, students should reflect on these questions before they speak: Is it true? Is it necessary? Is it kind? Teachers can also use the wheel of awareness as a tool to help students determine which emotions they should focus on. Students need to know that they do not have to become hostage to any one negative feeling.

Ninth graders and students in other transition grades may not have the social-emotional competencies for the school level they are about to enter. They are typically the students who get into trouble and face suspension or other disciplinary actions. There is no one-size-fits-all approach when it comes to SEL; it is dependent upon the school and its culture.

When managing behaviors, there must be consistency across classrooms and across school. The needs of each student are unique, and teachers should be mindful of this when implementing SEL in classrooms. Class rules that are simple and easy to remember are more effective and easier to enforce. Furthermore, students need brain breaks and reflections to foster their own well-being and self-awareness.

QUESTIONS FOR REFLECTION

1. How can teachers become effective role models for students in demonstrating it is all right to show emotion and to share vulnerability and feelings with others?
2. How can teachers best address mindfulness in their lessons?
3. How can teachers include reflections at the end of each lesson that provide space for student voices and attain student buy-in?

ANSWERS TO QUESTIONS FOR REFLECTION

Educators can become role models in showing students that it is all right to show emotion by doing so themselves. They can be willing to demonstrate their own vulnerability. They can take the time at the beginning of each class to discuss how everything is for them personally. They can model how to handle situations in a positive way.

Educators can best address mindfulness in their lessons by using an effective mindfulness curriculum and connecting content to students' personal feelings and life experiences/interests. Moreover, teachers can practice positive self-talk, which can be accomplished by initiating conversations about small accomplishments. They can consider improvising and failing without beating themselves up.

REFERENCES

Greenland, Susan Kaiser. 2010. *The Mindful Child: How to Help Your Kid Manage Stress and Become Happier, Kinder, and More Compassionate.* New York: Atria Paperback.

Siegel, Daniel J., and Tina Payne Bryson. 2012. *The Whole-Brain Child: 12 Revolutionary Strategies to Nurture Your Child's Developing Mind.* New York: Bantam.

PART II

Fostering Self-Management for Educators and Students

Chapter 3

Developing Self-Management for Educators

When educators are patient and compassionate with themselves and have strategies to reduce stress, they become more available for their students. It is impossible to build memories, engage in complex thoughts, or make meaningful decisions without emotion (Martinez Perez 2020). Emotions drive our attention; they influence our ability to process information and understand what we encounter. Educators can use their emotions in the decision-making process while incorporating better self-management. Emotions can become a tool in the self-management process.

TEACHERS AND SELF-MANAGEMENT

How can educators develop self-management skills within themselves to better serve their students? First, they can be organized. It helps to have premade lessons from previous years to refer to as well as a paper or electronic lesson planner. Writing reflection notes and/or updating the lessons for improvements can help educators address issues in real time. When educators model self-management, they are helping their students understand the importance of being organized, meeting deadlines, and efficiently managing their workloads. As Hobbes suggested, this preparation will groom them for the demands of careers and social life.

Teachers cannot expect students to have skills that they do not possess themselves. If educators appear to be unprepared for lessons, the students know it, and they take advantage of that lack of preparation. It is a self-management skill to be prepared with the right resources, activities, and engagement to keep students and educators on track. Nonetheless, if lessons take longer than expected or if there are technological issues, educators can demonstrate flexibility in dealing with these challenges by being truthful with their students about what is happening during the lesson.

Self-management is not just about organization, meeting deadlines, and appearing put-together for students; it is about staying true to one's own teaching style and celebrating our differences in small ways. Therefore, a teacher cannot automatically replicate a lesson verbatim that is not their own. Every teacher places their own creativity, uniqueness, and spin on each lesson.

There is a relationship between a teacher's behaviors, beliefs, and self-efficacy in terms of their subject knowledge and student achievement. One way in which teachers can instill their own behaviors into a classroom is to establish a positive classroom climate (Muijs and Reynolds 2002).

Transitions need to be short, learning must be organized, and lessons must start on time. Rules for student behavior should be addressed early in the year and clearly understood by students. Any negative student behavior should be corrected instantly, accurately, and constructively (Muijs and Reynolds 2002). In the meantime, it is crucial to demonstrate high expectations with enthusiasm.

Teacher self-efficacy affects not only the achievements but also the motivation of the students. It includes the educator's ability to self-manage during lesson delivery, including starting on time, transitioning well, and engaging students. Scaffolding can increase student achievement (Zee and Koomen 2016), and teachers can help students of all levels to expand upon their thinking. When teachers ensure equal engagement of students in all competency levels, they stop demonstrating favoritism, which can cause weaker student-teacher connections.

When educators and students practice self-management, they are in better shape for success. Educators need self-management to stay on track with their curriculum guides, deadlines, and more. Students need to know that their actions have consequences and that the teacher is prepared to deliver high-quality lessons with ease and care.

Teachers can refine their personal goals and effectively use multiple strategies such as breathing and mindfulness activities to create a positive connection with students. Teachers can use stress-reduction techniques to implement SEL more effectively. They can do this by modeling positive emotional regulation behaviors to help students monitor and control their own emotions (Yoder 2014).

DISRUPTIONS TO LEARNING

There are multiple vicious cycles that cause dynamic self-reinforcing problems for teachers and students during the learning process (Watkins 2003). They are outlined here in seven examples for teachers to recognize and avoid.

1. *Riding off in all directions where one cannot focus.* This is a mental lockup where one feels overwhelmed and has too many tasks where prioritization cannot occur. The educator is pulled from task to task and forced to constantly put out fires.
2. *Undefended boundaries.* Allowing anyone to take whatever one is able to offer can create a vicious cycle that causes anger and resentment. This can happen, for example, when an educator is tutoring students after school and does not have enough time to grade assignments or plan lessons. Setting up specific office hours or taking a break from tutoring can help teachers to regain equilibrium.
3. *Brittleness or uncertainty in transitions that breeds rigidity and defensiveness.* When educators are overly rigid, it can break students and disempower them from learning and doing quality work.
4. *Isolation, or not making the right connections with students.* When a teacher either does not take the time or simply does not have the time to create connections with students, this can discourage them from sharing critical information. Isolation causes poor decision-making, which can damage the teacher's credibility and further reinforce educator isolation.
5. *Biased judgment.* The tendency to focus on information that confirms your beliefs and filter out what does not can cloud your judgment. There is vulnerability and uncertainty in this course of action because of increased ambiguity and unpredictable emotions.
6. *Work avoidance.* This is the process of delaying work due to stress and being overwhelmed that lead to a vicious cycle.
7. *Going over the top without being able to accomplish goals due to high levels of stress.* This is essentially trying to accomplish more tasks than one person can handle at one given time, which as a teacher or as an administrator can occur at any moment.

All these vicious cycles can generate dangerous levels of stress. It is true that we all do need some stress to be productive: As you first begin to experience pressure, you are more productive. But too much stress can cause burnout. When this happens to teachers, the result is often that they work harder but achieve less (Watkins 2003).

PRIORITY SETTING FOR EDUCATORS

As educators, we need to set priorities, create plans, and direct actions to build momentum. To be successful in the classroom, we need personal disciplines that propel us in a productive direction. Consulting with others to determine your own weaknesses and strengths can will stimulate your thinking about your own routines and how you may be able to achieve them (Watkins 2003).

- *Plan to plan.* Do you devote time regularly, either daily or weekly, to plan work and reflect goals? At the end of each day, spend a few moments setting goals for the next day. Also do this at the end of the week. This practice will help you attain more control.
- *Defer commitment when you are able.* Do you regret commitments later? If so, make space for yourself and do not say yes to everything. Tell those asking for commitments from you that you need time to think about it.
- *Set aside time for hard work.* Do you devote time every day to your most important work? If you are too easily distracted, you need to set a chunk of independent work time aside for yourself every day. Eliminate distractions to help you accomplish your work.

SELF-REFLECTION FOR EDUCATORS

Self-reflection after each lesson is essential for personal growth and success. Potential questions for self-reflection include:

- How do you feel?
- Are you excited? Why, or why not?
- Are you confident? Why, or why not?
- What can you improve?
- Are you in control? If not, why not?
- What has bothered you so far?
- With which student(s) have you failed to connect?
- What has gone well? What has gone poorly?
- Which interactions could you address differently, and why?
- Which interactions exceeded your expectations, and why?
- Which of your choices turned out particularly well? Not so well? Why?

Save your responses to these questions so you can refer to them later to help you see developing patterns, the nature of the problems, and the quality of your interaction with them. After a couple of weeks, look back and reflect upon your reflections (Watkins 2003). What were your reactions to those issues? How can you improve upon your reactions and what can you do differently so that the issues they may cause with students and other staff do not continue? What missed opportunities do you regret the most? Are these issues situational or do they lie within you?

Foundations of self-efficacy involve systemic planning and disciplined execution. Solidifying your personal support systems can also help. Build a solid advice and a counsel network. You cannot do it all without the emotional and professional support from your peers (Watkins 2003). You always need a network of trusted educators who can easily identify with what you are going through. Having someone who fully understands the school culture, especially when you are a new teacher, is invaluable. However, they must have your best interests at heart.

It might be a struggle to achieve equilibrium every day, but it is essential to be successful and avoid burnout. Your success or failure is a result of the small decisions you make every day. Below is a final self-reflection checklist (Watkins 2003).

1. What are your greatest deficits and how do you compensate for them?
2. Which personal disciplines do you need most to create or improve? How will you accomplish that? What does your success look like?
3. What can you do to have more control over your environment?
4. How can you strengthen your advice-counsel network?

THE IMPORTANCE OF SLEEP AND HEALTHY HABITS

Improving sleep habits is just as important as self-management reflection techniques. It may sound basic, but quality sleep can provide the necessary energy to get through the day. According to Lipman and Parikh (2021), there are three types of chronotypes or natural preferences toward waking up and going to sleep. It is important to try to maximize your activities through your chronotype tendencies for optimal health and well-being. That way one can choose which rhythm best supports one's needs .

The first chronotype, which makes up 20 percent of the population, is the lark. Larks enjoy waking up early and have an abundance of energy in the morning. They typically wake up before 6 a.m., even without an alarm clock. Likewise, they naturally tend to get sleepy in the early evening, around 9 p.m. They are not overly reliant on caffeine during the morning hours. They are most productive and awake during the hours prior to lunch and lose their mental focus in the afternoon.

The second type is the owl, which also makes up about 20 percent of the population. Owls enjoy staying up past midnight. They wake up closer to 10 a.m. and prefer not to go to bed before 3 a.m. They need an alarm clock to wake up early and they tend to need caffeine to focus during the day. Their day starts during the afternoon, and their most productive hours are in the evening.

The last chronotype is the hummingbird, which makes up approximately 60 percent of the population. Hummingbirds are a mix of larks and owls, often having tendencies closer to one or the other.

Lipman and Parikh (2021) recommend that larks spend the late afternoon and evening engaging in outside activities such as going for a walk. If larks exercise, they should do so later in the day. It is essential for larks to socialize in the evening to reenergize toward the evening. For owls, Lipman and Parikh suggest dimming the lights in the evening, sleeping with the curtain open so the daylight will wake them up, and going for a walk as soon as they wake up. Owls should avoid sleeping in on the weekends, which causes social jet lag, and should not exercise or conduct stimulating activities in the evening. It is important for hummingbirds to recognize whether their tendencies shift more toward a lark or an owl and follow the appropriate suggestions to optimize productivity.

In addition to following the appropriate chronotype, it is important to avoid focusing on stress. When we overstress, we tend not to sleep. During the day, educators should attempt to not dwell on situations they cannot control, instead choosing to learn from these experiences and move forward.

Sleep patterns have changed significantly from the past. In the 1600s and earlier, people slept for four to five hours before waking, spent one to two hours in a meditative state, then slept again for four to five hours (Van Susteren and Colino 2020). If this type of sleep pattern is more natural to you, it may be worth considering revisiting the habits of our ancestors.

Movement of the body is beneficial to encouraging sleep. Consistent exercise and relaxation techniques such as meditation, yoga, and breathing exercises help the body stay calm and focused. All these activities encourage a reduction of stress. Often, we may feel as though we do not have time for these types of activities, but when we do not practice self-care, we tend to become overwhelmed with stress. This negatively impacts our ability to perform the duties of our jobs, which makes us feel inadequate.

The body also needs a balanced diet for exercise and relaxation, which play a vital role in our state of mind and our ability to process stressors that may come our way. Sugar, processed foods, and alcohol can cause inflammation and disrupt hormonal balance. Finding a rhythm that works for you is beneficial for reducing stress and encouraging sleep. Hence, following the chronotype examples can encourage a better rhythm.

EMOTIONS AND ORGANIZATION

Emotions drive our attention, and being more organized can help produce more positive emotions. Teachers should stay true to their own teaching style, because students can tell when they deviate from their natural tendencies, and it does not work well. Rousseau would suggest that staying true to one's own nature is best for both educators and students.

Teacher behaviors, beliefs, and self-efficacy are all interconnected. Self-efficacy involves time management and student engagement. For instance, good transitions into activities are essential for student comprehension, positive behaviors, and engagement. Educators should engage students equally in transition activities such as Spin the Wheel or Popsicle Sticks.

Stress and pressure negatively impact productivity. It is not pleasant for teachers to be overly rigid. Priorities should be set to build momentum, and setting goals for the next day at the end of each workday will allow room for more focus. Weekly lesson planning can help teachers more easily see the direction of their lesson plans and where they need to be adjusted. However, educators should not overly commit.

Teachers can stay up-to-date on school culture by speaking with someone who fully understands the culture of the school, particularly if they are a new teacher in the building. Dwelling on circumstances outside of one's control does not help well-being and can hurt sleep production. Accordingly, improving sleep by adjusting to natural body rhythms and sleep times optimizes health.

QUESTIONS FOR REFLECTION

1. How can better organization help teachers self-manage their classrooms more effectively?
2. How do teacher behaviors determine the classroom climate?
3. How can teachers improve their sleep rhythm to align with a healthier lifestyle?

ANSWERS TO QUESTIONS FOR REFLECTION

Improved organization can demonstrate to students that the teacher expects the same type of organization from them. Teacher behaviors influence classroom climate significantly. If teachers are approachable, students will feel safe and secure, making them more likely to feel comfortable sharing both content and personal information in class. Teachers must find time for a better sleep whenever they can, exercise regularly, and eat healthily to maintain a healthier lifestyle.

REFERENCES

Lipman, Frank, and Neil Parikh. 2021. *Better Sleep, Better You*. New York: Little Brown Spark.

Martinez Perez, Lorea. 2020. *Teaching with the Heart in Mind: A Complete Educator's Guide to Social Emotional Learning*. New York: Brisca Publishing.

Muijs, Daniel, and David Reynolds. 2002. "Teachers' Beliefs and Behaviors: What Really Matters?" *Journal of Classroom Interaction* 37, no. 2: 3–15.

Van Susteren, Lisa, and Stacey Colino. 2020. *Emotional Inflammation: Discover Your Triggers and Reclaim Your Equilibrium during Anxious Times*. Louisville, CO: Sounds True.

Watkins, Michael. 2003. *The First 90 Days: Proven Strategies for Getting up to Speed Faster and Smarter*. Boston: Harvard Business Review Press.

Yoder, Nicholas. 2014. *Self-Assessing Social and Emotional Instruction and Competencies: A Tool for Teachers*. Washington, DC: American Institutes for Research. Retrieved from https://files.eric.ed.gov/fulltext/ED553369.pdf.

Zee, Marjolein, and Helma M. Y. Koomen. 2016. "Teacher Self-Efficacy and Its Effects on Classroom Processes, Student Academic Adjustment, and Teacher Well-Being: A Synthesis of 40 Years of Research." *Review of Educational Research* 86, no. 4 (December): 981–1015.

Chapter 4

Developing Self-Management for Students

Students who are raised in challenging circumstances such as living in a single-parent household, with grandparents or other guardians, in group homes or foster homes, need extra support at school. Similarly, nowadays, many behavior issues that occur at school are linked to social media. Students commit suicide due to posts pertaining to school shootings, gender identity, bullying, and other complex life issues. Through relationships and mentorships, they learn self-awareness and self-management, and as a result, their self-efficacy increases. This indicates a strong need to adopt SEL in schools.

POSITIVE EXPECTATIONS

Teachers can instill self-management skills in their students by presenting them with positive expectations. They can demonstrate this simply by believing in their students and their ability to learn. Learners produce what the teachers expect of them. When a teacher expects a student to perform poorly, the student will do so because of the beliefs that are transferred to the student (Wong & Wong 2009). Likewise, if a teacher expects a student to be a high performer, that belief will be transferred to the student. This is why it is important for teachers to show the same positive expectations for all students.

While small cooperative group work allows students to interact directly with the content and master it, it is more engaging to teach the entire class instead of allowing students to work on worksheets or on their own schedules. Whole-class-directed instruction must be structured with objectives for the lesson, key points, and structured explanations (Muijs and Reynolds 2002). The lesson must have a summary activity so students understand the purpose behind their learning. The whole class should be interactive and lecture styles should be avoided.

Teachers can encourage student participation by asking them questions directly, using an appropriate wait time. These questions can be posed based on the level of difficulty (Muijs and Reynolds 2002). Moreover, students need immediate feedback not only to continue to grow but also to excel in the subject matter.

Varying teaching strategies allows teachers to address a variety of learners and their learning types (such as visual, auditory, reading/writing, and kinesthetic). While graphs and designs help visual learners, for example, songs facilitate the focused engagement of auditory learners. Textbook reading and written assignments are activities that help reading/writing learners. Kinesthetic learners benefit largely from activities such as four corners, review stations, labs, and acting.

Explanations should match the students' learning levels and can also be matched to the learner types in the classroom. Teachers can survey their students to find out the types of learners they have in their classes.

ENGAGEMENT

Materials and activities should be used to engage students. Asking students—even middle and high school students—to color is an excellent brain break, providing a way for them to self-soothe and reconnect. Choosing coloring sheets that can be related to the content makes the activity more relevant.

Another engagement activity is to have students role-play with puppets. Students can hide behind the puppets, which makes the activity easier, especially for students who are nervous or anxious about presenting. As Rousseau suggested, these engaging examples allow students to be children by resting their active brains. At the end of the school year, they may not remember the content, but they will remember the puppets.

Another way to give students a break is by asking them to stretch. Teachers can guide them through stretching or play a guiding video and stretch along with it, encouraging the students to do the same. This works best at the elementary levels, but it can be a method to engage willing middle school and high school students as well. Whatever the activity, it is beneficial for educators to find ways to provide their students breaks that will make it easier for them to continue their learning throughout the school day.

Teachers who are simply present and pay attention can help defuse unwanted behavioral issues. Teachers can observe whether students are paying attention to what they are doing. If they are paying attention, then they are less likely to misbehave. Instead of criticizing the behavior, teachers can guide students to address temporary situations that do not reflect who they are overall (Lemov 2015). This is a better solution to resolve unwanted behaviors without belittling students.

Having a highly engaging classroom is an effective way to manage misbehaviors. According to Marzano (2017), engagement is divided into four components:

1. Paying attention
2. Being energized
3. Being intrigued
4. Being inspired

Students must be mentally prepared to learn. Engagement is the gatekeeper to mental readiness (Marzano 2017). When students are engaged and inspired, they are more likely to walk away from the lesson with new knowledge.

A part of being knowledgeable about engagement as an educator is recognizing when the students are not engaged. The right approach is to actively engage students when it is appropriate. When students respond to an educator's questions, it indicates that they are engaged. Teachers can use this data to determine the engagement of their classes.

If people can change how they mentally represent a stimulus, they can exert self-control and escape from being victims of stimuli that control their behavior. This takes strong motivation and the best of intentions. An example of this is the marshmallow test, where a researcher provides preschool-aged children the option of one marshmallow now or two marshmallows later if they are willing to wait for a larger reward. Children who are willing to wait demonstrate higher self-control, which leads to improved later-life outcomes (Mischel 2014).

SELF-REGULATION

Self-regulation is the ability of a child to understand and safely manage strong emotions when they occur (Bilmes 2012). Emotions tend to rule behaviors, and to manage emotions, children need to first observe them. They can learn to recognize their emotions by first noticing how they feel. At the same time, children also must learn about the emotions of others. Learning how to regulate emotions takes practice and guidance from adults.

Classroom social skills are improved when teachers encourage self-monitoring in their students. Risk factors such as alcohol and drug abuse are reduced through prevention programs that instill self-management and problem-solving skills (Peterson et al. 2006). Structured learning can aid students in identifying the critical social skills that can be taught by modeling, role-playing, and feedback.

There is a strong need to demonstrate empathy by responding to feelings and needs of others (Bilmes 2012), and listening and paying attention to the emotions of others is essential. The greatest gift we can give others is to listen. As children self-regulate and identify feelings in themselves and others, they need to understand that these feelings change over time and are not permanent.

It is helpful for children to build an emotional vocabulary or use the mood meter. Examples of alternative words include annoyed, confused, generous, joyful, worried, bored, embarrassed, ignored, safe, calm, excited, and impatient (Bilmes 2012).

Walking breaks and other physical activities help students to self-regulate. Just like adults, children need this time to rebalance and work through their emotions. Educators can describe how an adult who has trouble managing impulses and emotions might behave, so that the students know it is not just children who suffer from these issues (Bilmes 2012).

In the marshmallow test, how children mentally represented external rewards predictably affected how long they waited for the marshmallows. Researchers in the experiment asked the participants what conditions would help them wait. This experiment allows us to see how children manage to delay and resist temptation and how differences in this ability play out over time (Mischel 2014). Experiments such as the marshmallow test are indicators that Hobbes would have endorsed because of the strong demand to delay gratification in work and in society.

Without adequate self-control skills, optimistic expectations, success experiences, and the support of others, children may remain largely controlled by their hot system (default) and are more likely to fail at mastery. Options shrink and they may have more feelings of helplessness rather than hopefulness (Mischel 2014).

In addition to mastering self-control, students also require an average of ten hours of sleep. Unfortunately, for many, the school day begins between 7:00 and 8:00 a.m., before students are ready to perform. Relatively few students are ready to learn prior to 8:30 a.m., yet, according to the National Sleep Foundation, 87 percent of high school students are required to do just that (Lipman and Parikh 2021).

THE NEED FOR ADEQUATE SLEEP FOR STUDENTS

Studies show that students who start school before 8:00 a.m. perform worse than those who start later in the day. Students who attend school later are more alert and not only earn higher test scores but also face fewer car accidents. Hence, it is a win-win situation for everyone—specifically for educators, parents, and students—to push back the start to the school day.

Educators and parents can ensure that children get a healthy amount of sleep so they can be successful in school, avoid accidents, and fight off depression. Inadequate sleep produces negative results in many aspects of the lives of both children and adults.

Sleep-deprived students experience more emotional and behavioral problems and have worse decision-making and impulse-control skills. Similarly, sleep deprived kids are more likely to perform worse academically and athletically (Lipman and Parikh 2021). Thus, for improved student well-being, it is important to encourage school leadership to push back the school day to encourage more sleep.

Students need to be provided the opportunity to talk about themselves. This makes them feel valued and more likely to do their work. They need to feel welcome in the classroom. When students hear stories from their peers, they feel inspired to make a change in their own lives. Likewise, when they communicate about themselves to others, they develop a more positive self-image simply through their desire to share what they are passionate about or what they believe in (Marzano 2017).

SELF-ACTUALIZATION

Students naturally engage more in class when the teachers attempt to make real-world connections with their personal interests along with the content (Marzano 2017). When students explain how these connections make a difference for them, they better understand the content, making them more likely to describe a class as relevant to them personally.

Self-actualization is having a connection with a higher purpose, and students can achieve it by having long-term goals (Marzano 2017). Their goals could be making a particular team, going to college, or getting high grades. Teachers can set aside time for students to work on their goals.

Moreover, teachers can ask their students to pursue altruistic projects, which allow them to work on activities that benefit others (Marzano 2017). Students can volunteer and report what they have learned from their experience. These types of projects build meaningful community relationships that benefit both the students and the community.

Like any extrinsic motivator, goals narrow the focus, since they force the mind to concentrate on a specific outcome. Pink (2009) suggests that goals can motivate everyone to try harder, work longer, and achieve more. That is why teachers, coaches, and parents advise that setting goals and working to achieve them make a difference.

GOAL SETTING AND MOTIVATION

Pink discusses extrinsic and intrinsic motivation in elucidating terms. For right-brain activities such as critical thinking and creativity, contingent rewards can be damaging. Intrinsic motivation—the drive to do something that is interesting, challenging, and absorbing—is essential for artists, scientists, inventors, and students (Pink 2009). Unfortunately, the conditional motivators that drive many businesses and schools deter rather than promote creativity.

Goals work in the long term. When students put their minds to meeting goals, they are more likely to achieve them. Goal-setting worksheets are an excellent tool to use for this, helping students set goals and reflect upon whether their goals were achieved. Encourage students to set weekly, monthly, quarterly, and yearly goals for anything, whether related to the content or outside of it, such as obtaining a driver's license or a permit.

TAKEAWAYS FOR STUDENT SELF-MANAGEMENT

More students than ever live within nontraditional family structures, and these students increasingly need more support. Their self-efficacy increases through positive adult relationships, and teachers present positive expectations when they believe in their students.

The students are engaged and the whole class is taught better when teachers use interesting activities rather than only worksheets. Summary activities such as exit tickets and reflections allow prior instruction to connect to current and future instruction. Both students and teachers need to know where their learning is headed so they can better address gaps in learning together. Having students involved in the learning direction process further encourages learning.

There are different types of learners, and they require a variety of activities. All students can benefit from brain break activities where they can go on a walk, stretch, or simply listen to music. These small brain breaks make it easier to focus and to stay focused for longer periods of time without energy drain.

Self-monitoring should be encouraged. Students can learn about the emotions of others while also monitoring their own. Furthermore, teachers can demonstrate empathy by acknowledging the emotional needs of others. This modeling will help students provide the same empathy to their peers. Helping students build an emotional vocabulary through the mood meter allows educators and students to be more present in the moment. The ability to label emotions aids in diffusing behavioral problems.

Educators can inspire. Assessments and check-ins such as the marshmallow test allow educators to see the students' ability to delay gratification. Encouraging students to delay external rewards and practice self-control will serve them better later in life.

Students need a higher purpose and long-term goals. There needs to be more of a focus on developing intrinsic motivation in education, recognizing that high test scores and grades are not the only rewards. Intrinsic motivation is a more powerful tool to motivate students to follow their dreams and will keep them grounded in their self-discovery. On the other hand, extrinsic motivation can work well for short-term goals.

QUESTIONS FOR REFLECTION

1. How can teacher relationships with students improve student self-management?
2. What can teachers do to engage their students in effective goal setting?
3. What can teachers do to engage students in a self-management practice?

ANSWERS FOR REFLECTION

Teacher relationships with students can improve student self-management. Teachers can engage their students in effective goal setting by modeling and teaching how to set goals. They can set goals together at the beginning of the school year and revisit them regularly. To engage students in a self-management practice, teachers can encourage them to find accountability partners. Once they are comfortable with self-managing themselves, students can discontinue the use of accountability partners.

REFERENCES

Bilmes, Jenna. 2012. *Beyond Behavior Management: The Six Life Skills Children Need.* 2nd ed. St. Paul, MN: Redleaf Press.

Lemov, Doug. 2015. *Teach Like a Champion 2.0: 62 Techniques That Put Students on the Path to College.* San Francisco: Joseey-Bass.

Lipman, Frank, and Neil Parikh. 2021. *Better Sleep, Better You*. New York: Little Brown Spark.

Marzano, Robert J. 2017. *The New Art and Science of Teaching*. Bloomington, IN: Solution Tree.

Mischel, Walter. 2014. *The Marshmallow Test: Mastering Self-Control*. New York: Little, Brown.

Muijs, Daniel, and David Reynolds. 2002. "Teachers' Beliefs and Behaviors: What Really Matters?" *Journal of Classroom Interaction* 37, no. 2: 3–15.

Peterson, Lloyd Douglas, K. Richard Young, Charles L. Salzberg, Richard P. West, and Mary Hill. 2006. "Using Self-Management Procedures to Improve Classroom Social Skills in Multiple General Education Settings." *Education and Treatment of Children* 29, no. 1 (February): 1–21.

Pink, Daniel H. 2009. *Drive: The Surprising Truth about What Motivates Us*. New York: Riverhead.

Wong, Harry K., and Rosemary T. Wong. 2009. *The First Days of School: How to Be an Effective Teacher*. Mountain View, CA: Harry K. Wong Publications.

PART III

Enhancing Responsible Decision-Making for Educators and Students

Chapter 5

Strengthening Responsible Decision-Making for Educators

Students tend to do their work better when teachers show they care about their students. Educators must go into classrooms understanding that conflict is inevitable, and it will always be a part of the learning process to receive pushback from both students and parents.

Good behavior must be taught and retaught consistently and systematically. Students' behavior can be changed when they are shown how to make the necessary changes, whether gradually or immediately. Since the classroom environment can have a significant impact on student success, teachers do have the power to set up classrooms that promote student success rather than hinder it.

When making decisions, we cannot treat a new problem like an old one. To utilize resources of intelligence and courage, we must consider the problem as an extraordinary and exceptional occurrence (Hammond 2001). Just like anyone else, educators need boundary conditions to be met for effective decision making. Consider the following questions:

1. What are the objectives the decision must reach?
2. What are the minimum goals it must attain?
3. What are the conditions it must satisfy?

The more alternatives and objectives one pursues, the more trade-offs one must make. The practice of trial and error is the most widely used approach for adapting partial knowledge. Tentativeness, or the commitment to revise one's course of action if necessary, is a good approach to take. When educators find an effective intervention, they can study the outcomes to appropriately adjust the intervention. Before deciding something does not work, teachers should try it for a short period of time before changing course (Hammond 2001).

Procrastination is the delay of a decision until the data are in or additional data are reviewed. Procrastination occurs when someone is not eager to decide, perhaps needing more information to proceed or out of discomfort making the decision under the circumstances.

Decision staggering is a form of procrastination in decision-making that can be adjusted incrementally (Hammond 2001). Instead of making the larger decision at once, one may prefer to stagger the decision-making process, dividing the larger decision into manageable steps to make smaller decisions one at a time.

The ultimate combination of procrastinating and decision staggering is fractionalizing. Fractionalizing is spreading a single intervention over time with sub-decisions that can be staggered (Hammond 2001). This includes making small portions of a decision without committing to the larger decision. This process can be spread over a long period to avoid making the larger decision until the person is prepared to do so. An individual who is flexible or cautious in capacity can proceed to making the decision with partial knowledge.

DECISION-MAKING AND EMOTIONS

Our emotions and feelings are essential in our intuitive ability to make good decisions. Balanced emotions are crucial to intuitive decision-making (Hammond 2001). It is important to be willing to change decisions; do not fall in love with your decisions, because you may need to change them.

People who structure choices create a backdrop for decision-making. Teachers who are natural choice architects can influence the quality of decisions of the students (Mauboussin 2013). How we feel about something influences our decisions, so teachers must be cognizant of how their feelings are affecting the colleagues and students around them.

An important axiom is "Practice makes permanent, not perfect." When students feel comfortable making mistakes, they are more likely to persevere and excel in whatever they do. A simple callout for students—such as, "If you can't make a mistake," with the student response, "you can't do anything"— is an excellent way to motivate students to keep trying even if they fail.

EXTERNAL FACTORS WITH DECISION-MAKING

Effective teachers notice subtle mannerisms, body, language, and tone (Dahlgren and Hyatt 2007). They know when their students are not all right and how to use effective teaching strategies to redirect students. Educators can ask students to look around the room and see who is not doing their work. Motivated students can persuade the distracted students to pay attention in class or to get back on task, putting the onus back on the students. They become responsible for their own learning, which is ultimately the best.

It is also important for educators to pay attention when deciding where to place posters and decor in the classroom (Dahlgren and Hyatt 2007). Decorative items should not compete with materials placed for instructional purposes. Learning is an arduous task, and students may be inadvertently distracted from their assignments by beautiful pictures on the wall. It is necessary to arrange the room so that the instructional area stands out. Assignments and even tests can include something silly, which will help keep students engaged with their work without being distracted. They are more likely to do their work when they are happy and engaged.

Kids are going through so much more now than ever before. The lack of a true human connection and the preoccupation of many adults in their lives with devices can mean many students' basic needs are not fulfilled, making it difficult for them to focus on the content. When serving students, educators need to focus on Maslow's hierarchy of needs before Bloom's taxonomy. (A simple way to remember this is "Maslow before Bloom.")

Teachers learn classroom management repeatedly on the job, not in teacher preparation programs. Trust is the first thing teachers should focus on is classroom norms. Another way teachers can build relationships and foster effective classroom management is by getting to know the students well.

Keeping a private observation journal and taking five to ten minutes each day to write observations of at least one student is a way to gather information about students (Corliss and Dahlgren 2018). The student's name, date, and observation will provide a reference point for later as a self-check-in to determine whether the teacher is dividing their attention fairly between all students.

There are multiple problems that hinder the process of responsible decision-making for educators. The need to teach online as well as hybrid/concurrent classes has been taxing on teachers who are not accustomed to this type of teaching. In some educators, this delivery method may have caused cybersickness, a term coined during the pandemic to refer to the effects of the constant movements and action of being on a screen. The live games that provide a fun way to interact with students have also been taxing on educator well-being.

One way educators (and parents) can effectively deal with students is simply to listen (Faber and Mazlish 1980). Acknowledging students' needs and feelings in a constructive way allows them to feel validated and trust the educator. When students make a complaint or a statement that the teacher disagrees with, it is important to avoid immediately arguing with the statement.

Rather, simply saying, "I understand how you feel" or "I understand why you would say that" show that the adult is not immediately disregarding something that seems unreasonable.

BEHAVIORS AND DECISION-MAKING

Avoiding immediate angry reactions to a misbehavior leads to a faster diffusion of the situation. When the teacher stays calm and focused, without allowing disruptions to completely take a class off the rails, it helps everyone—including the teacher. It is essential to keep calm and provide a positive example to the other students, who are looking up to the teacher as a role model in difficult situations.

When dealing with difficult behaviors, it is important for educators to keep in mind how the misbehaviors may affect the students who demonstrate positive behaviors. The last thing an educator wants is to lose the students who are good role models. Listening and acknowledging feelings in students will reduce arguments and outbursts.

Educators can provide names for the feelings their students have and provide them with a creative way to express their wishes through fantasy (Faber and Mazlish 1980). It is an easy solution to say to a child, "You wish you had. . . . " This sentence starter validates their feelings while letting them know that the adult is listening.

Role-plays are also an excellent way to achieve this goal, especially for younger students. Students can be tasked with creating a dialogue with other students and acting out how they may achieve their wishes or goals. This is particularly effective with money management activities, world language classes, and the humanities.

TEACHER VULNERABILITY

Educators should feel comfortable sharing their feelings with their students, too. This vulnerability makes the students more likely to identify with their teachers. Sharing feelings shows courage and trust, and it encourages empathy in students toward their educators. Many students do not see their teachers as adults with lives outside of school. It is hard for them to imagine that teachers have other responsibilities. Choosing to be honest and open with students allows students to see that teachers are affected by their lives outside of school, just like the students' outside lives affect them.

Addressing alternative solutions to punishment, Faber and Mazlish (1980) provide the following steps:

1. Point out a way to be helpful.
2. Express strong disapproval (without attacking character).
3. State your expectations.
4. Show the child how to make amends.
5. Offer a choice.
6. Take action.
7. Allow the child to experience the consequences of his or her misbehavior.

It is ultimately more beneficial for both the educator and the student when the educator acknowledges the student's struggle instead of giving classic punishments. To encourage autonomy in students, educators should let them make choices without asking too many questions or rushing to answer questions, encourage students to use outside sources, and do not take away hope (Faber and Mazlish 1980). Furthermore, teachers need to understand of resilience-building practices for students so they can help the students be more responsible in making sound decisions.

To provide adequate praise and encouragement, teachers can describe what they see and what they feel, summarizing the student's praiseworthy behavior with a few words (Faber and Mazlish 1980). It is not enough to provide short one-word praise such as "good," "great," and "amazing."

SETTING STUDENTS UP FOR SUCCESS

Students need to hear descriptions of their positive behaviors so they know exactly what they did right, which motivates them to do it again. They will not know what specifically was "good" if that is all that they are told. Educators should be purposeful with their words to encourage continued positive behaviors that benefit the entire class as well as the student producing the improved behavior.

Students should be liberated from playing specific roles they are accustomed to hearing for themselves, such as a "stubborn child" (Faber and Mazlish 1980). To do this, educators must look for opportunities to demonstrate that students can have a new vision of themselves. Students can be placed into situations where they see themselves differently. It benefits students to hear their teacher say something positive about them. Educators should model the behaviors that are found in a positive classroom environment. Whenever students returns to their old misbehaviors, educators can restate expectations and ask them how the misbehavior made them feel.

When educators consider balancing the needs and behaviors of the entire class, they are better able to meet the goals and expectations of learning for the day. Collaboration with colleagues can help solve problems that may not initially be evident. Staying consistent and focused is essential because students know when treatments are unfair and will call their teachers out on it. It is essential to regularly work to find an equilibrium between students' emotional and academic needs (Yoder 2014).

CULTURALLY RESPONSIVE TEACHING

Teachers can use classroom management as a mechanism to connect and build trusting relationships with their students. Increasingly, teachers need examples of ways to integrate SEL and culturally responsive teaching (CRT) into their practice (Stevenson and Markowitz 2019). Trust derives from respect; when teachers trust the natural wisdom of children, as Rousseau proposed, children are more inclined to trust their educators.

CRT is a pedagogy that recognizes the importance of integrating students' cultural references into their learning (Ladson-Billings 1994). Unfortunately, few teacher preparation programs offer examples and ideas to integrate SEL and CRT, which have become essential in education.

CRT and SEL can be best implemented into learning through building trust by understanding students' background and culture. Teachers should survey students to understand their backgrounds and cultural differences. This information can be used to tailor instruction to student needs and interests in a culturally responsive manner.

To make classrooms more equitable, schools need to move away from many of the traditional grading practices, reminiscent of the Industrial Revolution, designed to keep students' behavior in line and make them ready for the factory line (Feldman 2019). For teachers to approach their students in more equitably and social-emotionally friendly ways, they need to rethink their approaches to minimum grading policies, group work grading, extra credit, cheating, homework, retakes on assessments, and rubrics.

Minimum grading policies provide students a score of 50 percent even if they did not submit an assignment. They can also receive the 50 percent if they receive a score below that benchmark on the assignment. Mathematically speaking, it is very difficult for a child to catch up after suffering from low grades at the beginning of the year (Feldman 2019).

Minimum grading policies have mostly been used in urban schools to help bolster the grades of all students equitably, but they gained wider popularity during the pandemic. While this may be a relatively new concept in the United States, minimum grading policies are more common in other parts of the world. For example, all of New Zealand uses the 50 percent minimum grading policy, and boys—who make up 90 percent of the student population—mostly benefit from this policy (Feldman 2019). Although decisions about school- or district-wide policies are not up to individual teachers, classroom teachers can institute their own minimum grading policies and suggest them to colleagues.

The concept of minimum grading can be particularly difficult and possibly threatening for teachers because they feel that it could diminish their authority, perceiving that such a grading policy weakens their power and influence over student behavior. On the contrary, minimum grading empowers teachers and schools. It neutralizes the negativities of grading in school learning (Feldman 2019). It improves behavior and creates a climate for caring, hopeful, and supportive adults who wish to see their students grow and develop skills. This is a key step to fostering a caring culture in a classroom, a school, or a school district.

When teachers assign group work for a grade—be it a project, a presentation, or a group quiz—each student should be provided separate grades instead of a group grade. Group work allows students to practice their collaboration skills and many other SEL qualities.

Extra credit is not equitable and should not be given because it is not a true reflection of students' grades. Students rely on extra credit as a cushion, but it allows them to escape from doing the real work where actual learning takes place. Extra credit does not teach SEL skills or content area knowledge; in fact, it teaches students that they can be rewarded with extrinsic reward points for simple actions such as bringing extra paper and Kleenex to school or answering bonus fun questions on a quiz or an exam (Feldman 2019).

When students cheat, the most equitable and SEL-friendly approach is restitution practices, which state that the person who is responsible for the negative action must do something to make the victim "whole" again (Feldman 2019). For a student, this can be a compensation for the damage caused to the class and the educator. Cheating students should be given a second chance to take the quiz while the teacher monitors them. The student who cheated could be assigned a classroom responsibility such as passing out papers. Another option is to ask the student to apologize to the class.

Homework is another aspect of educator expectations that is not equitable (Feldman 2019). Of course, there are classes where homework is more important. Unfortunately, homework may not be feasible for students who work, care for siblings, or participate in multiple extracurricular activities. Many students in these situations copy other students' work because they simply do not have the time. Some students may even forget to submit their assignments.

All students deserve a caring adult who would like to see them achieve high results. Educators should motivate students to achieve academic success by supporting them to cultivate a growth mindset and giving them opportunities for redemption (Feldman 2019). Retakes on assessments are equitable only when they are mandatory for all students who scored poorly. Unfortunately, many teachers do not have the time and energy to address all students who perform poorly on assessments. What educators can do is to recognize the issues with equity in retakes and do the best they can to offer all students the opportunity to retake assessment on which they scored poorly. Simply announcing that retakes are available for an assessment can be enough for educators who are crunched for time.

Even for driving tests, college assignments, and credentialing certificate exams such as the professional exams for teachers, lawyers, and nurses allow for retakes. When educators announce that there are no options to retake an assessment, it teaches students that the world does not allow retakes in life, which is not the truth.

Rubrics are a great way to aid students in understanding how they are being evaluated. They are an equitable way to help students understand how teachers assign grades and to understand how they can improve their grades. They also allow teachers to see more clearly if there is any implicit bias in their grading approach (Feldman 2019).

To change our schools to be more equitable is to align our schools, our instruction, and the learning environments of our students (Feldman, 2019). There are many reasons to avoid changing approaches to grading, such as the lack of resources, time, and energy. Unfortunately, if these approaches do not change, we are only hindering our students from being successful in the right-brain, conceptual-thinking world, where the best available jobs, now and in the future, exist.

TAKEAWAYS FOR EDUCATOR RESPONSIBLE DECISION-MAKING

The reflection process to do this work effectively is arduous but well worth the effort for the benefit of students and educators alike. No one wants to feel as though they have been cheated out of the education they rightfully deserve because of the century-old practices designed to prepare the students for factory work.

To follow both Hobbes's and Rousseau's methods concurrently, the goal for educators is to build an informed citizenry that is empathetic to others. Educators are expected to simultaneously prepare children for society and society for children.

When we all show more kindness to one another, it is easier to meet challenges as they arise. Educators need the tools to help promote kindness in their classroom, whether it is through SEL, CRT, PBIS, MTSS, or other disciplines. When all aspects of the child are addressed in the classroom, no matter the context, children are validated and encouraged.

Teachers are held accountable for more than ever before. Teachers feel as though parents are not doing as much as they should in parenting; unfortunately, some parents are working multiple jobs and do not have the bandwidth to address concerns as they did in previous generations.

Teachers are expected to help students perform well on assessments, especially focusing on teaching for standardized testing. It has been suggested that teachers provide lesson plans for the entire school year at the beginning of every year. The issue of standardized testing has been around for quite some time, ever since No Child Left Behind and the reallocation of resources to wealthier schools as a reward for high performance. Teachers have long felt the pressure to motivate their students to perform well on tests, particularly standardized assessments required of the states where they teach.

Educators understand that if their students do not perform well, they will lose funding, along with their ability to provide the best education possible for the learners. This constant reward-and-punishment system for student performance on state standardized testing is demoralizing, but it is a part of the current education system of the United States. Teachers must constantly be flexible and learn the ins and outs of upcoming assessments for their students, and ultimately, for their schools.

Without their constant effort in shaping the excellence of their students, the very schools that now have resources will not have them in the future. The teachers who are fighting for their students in schools that lack resources are doing all they can to provide the best they can for their student population. It is an unfair system that rewards the strong and punishes the weak. All educators can do is to understand the system and do the best they can do given the set of circumstances that they are in—without blaming themselves.

There is a lack of support for educator professional development, especially when it comes to disconnected students who need SEL. Not all schools provide educators the necessary training to address these important, life-changing skills. There are many anxious students who refuse to interact with educators and their peers because they do not remember or know how to interact in a classroom setting.

Teacher salaries are low all over the country, and many need to work multiple jobs or have side hustles to make ends meet. They face all these challenges while making between three thousand and forty-five hundred decisions per day to address the needs of a wide variety of learners (Dahlgren and Hyatt 2007). That is why educators are so exhausted. Additionally, teachers may not always know how to handle kids who refuse to do what they have been asked to do.

Accountability is essential, both within and outside of the classroom. If one cannot measure something or manage it, then it should not be taught. Just like the content, SEL should be measured using student and teacher surveys to assess whether true learning is taking place. This measurement keeps schools and school systems accountable for topics and skills that need to be taught.

Students are more likely to do their work when they can see that their teacher cares. Conflict is inevitable. Before trying a different approach or moving on to write reflections on how the approach went, educators can first test out the approach that is available to them. The willingness to change decisions when needed is essential. Instructing students that it is all right to make mistakes allows them to learn in a more natural way. An observation journal can aid with making decisions to address issues such as the equal distribution of attention among all students during instruction.

Students' essential needs must be met before effective instruction can occur. When students lash out, it is important to avoid immediate reactions. Many times, students are seeking a reaction from their teacher and there is no other reason for the misbehavior occurred. Educators can acknowledge students' struggles before punishing them. For instance, an educator could share a simple affirming statement such as, "I understand that you do not want to take a test today, but it will help me determine what I still need to teach you." It is equally important to acknowledge positive behavior so that students understand how they should behave.

CRT is a method that incorporates students' cultural references and allows them to feel a sense of belonging at school. This connection is important if positive learning experiences are to occur. Equity can be achieved through multiple policies. These include minimum grading policies, the elimination of unnecessary homework tasks, the avoidance of extra credit, a focus on grading individual rather than group work efforts, the ability to retake exams, rubrics to understand evaluation, and retrospective practices to address cheating.

Modern schools have existed for just over a century. Due to the ever-changing needs of school environments, teachers require more support. The recommendations discussed in this chapter are holistic strategies to address behavior issues, equity concerns, and responsible decision-making in the classroom.

QUESTIONS FOR REFLECTION

1. How can teachers provide constructive feedback that is useful for students but does not take too much time?
2. How can alternate methods of punishment improve instruction and learning?

3. How can teachers encourage autonomy in their students?

ANSWERS TO QUESTIONS FOR REFLECTION

Teachers can provide useful constructive feedback without taking too much time by giving assignments that are more meaningful and concise. Assignments should be specific and direct, with clear instructions and rubrics. Alternate methods of punishment improve instruction because they send the message that punishment is not meant to hurt students but to hold them accountable to their community. Finally, teachers can encourage autonomy in their students by encouraging student agency and informing them well about classroom policies.

REFERENCES

Corliss, Julia Candace, and Aaron Dahlgren. 2018. *Unconditional Positive Regard: The Science, Psychology, and Strategies behind High-Performing Classrooms.* Hayden Lake, ID: Center for Teacher Effectiveness.

Dahlgren, Rick, and Judy Hyatt. 2007. *Time to Teach: Encouragement, Empowerment, and Excellence in Every Classroom with Refocus.* Hayden Lake, ID: Center for Teacher Effectiveness.

Faber, Adele, and Elaine Mazlish. 1980. *How to Talk So Kids Will Listen & Listen So Kids Will Talk.* New York: Scribner.

Feldman, Joe. 2019. *Grading for Equity: What It Is, Why It Matters, and How It Can Transform Schools and Classrooms.* Thousand Oaks, CA: Corwin.

Hammond, Zaretta L. 2014. *Culturally Responsive Teaching and the Brain: Promoting Authentic Engagement and Rigor among Culturally and Linguistically Diverse Students.* Thousand Oaks, CA: Corwin.

Ladson-Billings, Gloria. 1994. *The Dreamkeepers: Successful Teachers of African American Children.* San Francisco: Jossey-Bass.

Mauboussin, Michael J. 2013. *Think Twice: Harnessing the Power of Counterintuition.* Boston: Harvard Business Review Press.

Stevenson, Heidi, and Nancy Lourié Markowitz. 2019. "Introduction: Social Emotional Learning and Culturally Responsive and Sustaining Teaching Practices." *Teacher Education Quarterly* 46, no. 4 (Fall): 3–9.

Yoder, Nicholas. 2014. *Self-Assessing Social and Emotional Instruction and Competencies: A Tool for Teachers.* Washington, DC: American Institutes for Research. Retrieved from https://files.eric.ed.gov/fulltext/ED553369.pdf.

Chapter 6

Strengthening Responsible Decision-Making for Students

Psychologists have long known that warm, open, caring responses encourage others to discuss their problems before they cause significant issues. Teachers who display self-control, respect for their students, good manners, courtesy, honesty, fairness, and good judgment teach by example. They strive to create a safe classroom climate, provide plenty of feedback, respect individuality and personal integrity, be flexible and fair, be firm when necessary, and welcome creativity and imagination (Dahlgren and Hyatt 2007).

RESPECT FOR STUDENTS

All effective teachers show respect for their students. Students need to feel known, liked, and respected before they can openly interact with teachers and respond to instruction. Current researchers widely accept the premise that self-esteem is significantly associated with personal satisfaction and effective functioning (Dahlgren and Hyatt 2007). Teachers who merely explain the rules without engaging the students in active learning tend to become frustrated with the outcome.

In inviting students to help write classroom rules, for example, teachers do not give away their powers of final decision-making and enforcement (Dahlgren and Hyatt 2007). Rather, they must exercise their power to revise the rules if necessary and to enforce the class rules throughout the year.

On rare occasions, teachers have been known to use this same power to make inappropriate requests of students. Such examples include requiring students to obey any request, no matter how unreasonable, from a teacher; prohibiting students to question the teacher's authority; or applying inconsistent/unfair rules regarding expectations, grading policies, and submission of assignments.

Icebreakers can be used to put learners in the mood to learn. Learning is more pleasant in a lighthearted atmosphere. Students are more likely to retain information after a good laugh. Everyone, including teachers, will enjoy the educational process when humor is a part of it.

Learning to take ownership of one's life choices is of great benefit to both students and society. When children learn how to meet high expectations for behavior and come to believe in their own ability to change their behavioral patterns, they begin to feel an honest pride in their own accomplishments (Dahlgren and Hyatt 2007).

The SEL views in practice start with the school leaders or the administration. A goal for teachers is to consider both academic concepts—the skills or content they want the students to know—and the related SEL competencies while planning instruction. During the lesson-planning process, teachers should consider how they can use academic skills as a tool to get students to learn or apply a related SEL skill.

Students need SEL skills to recover from negativity. An increasing source of negativity is rapidly evolving through online platforms. Technology has changed the way students develop in the modern world, largely due to their near-constant access to new technologies and devices.

Higher awareness of SEL may yield higher engagement among students when trying to master a subject matter. To target students with SEL, teachers may decide to develop encompassing questions that help students connect with the topics they have previously seen, done, or heard about. As students read, they must be able to connect a piece of the text or annotation to something that they already know about or are familiar with. This is the teacher's attempt to connect text to life.

RELEVANT CLASS DISCUSSIONS

Discussions about current events, such as recent nationwide school shootings, provide opportunities for the class to go off topic yet still be engaged in SEL learning. Teachers can engage their classes if they spend time discussing real-world events that affect their students' daily lives. The students may not be open about the content, but they may be willing to discuss their opinions on such topics as school shootings.

Teachers can share similar stories of how bomb threats were the norm during their own high school years. They can ask engaging questions of their students, such as, "Why are schools nationwide doing a walkout?" The teacher can probe the students with questions such as, "Are there fifteen to twenty people who you speak to on a regular basis? And if not, think about why not?"

Teachers can also initiate discussions about the activities students do outside of school that are related to schoolwork. These are agreeable ways to keep a class engaged in SEL. For example, such conversations can be started by asking, "Which clubs are you involved in, if any?" Genuine heart-to-heart chats, where the students sense that they have a voice and that their teacher cares about what they do both inside and outside of the classroom, are just as valuable as teaching the content—in fact, they can make teaching the content easier.

METHODS TO CONNECT WITH STUDENTS

Classes such as math are unique because of the technicality of the subject matter. Keeping an animated voice that fluctuates in tone helps teachers connect with students by keeping them focused on what the educator is saying. The focus can be on the content, and then—of course, together with that—teachers may use analogies and examples that are relevant to the students. Jokes can also act as great motivators and connectors for educators in such situations.

Nonetheless, depending on class culture, teachers can still be tough with the students; for example, explaining that there are natural consequences for not reading directions clearly and helping students generate possible solutions to prevent the predicament in the future. It is essential to practice and reteach the selected solution, since learners require repeated practice of all new skills to maintain them.

Math teachers should broadly use real-world examples to engage students. When explaining polynomials, the example of owing someone a dollar can make the concept more applicable and to expand it beyond more than just numbers. Another relatable example when solving polynomials is to ask anecdotally, "Can someone (numbers) make the king and queen happy so that you can invite them to the castle?" Such activities that personify difficult concepts make math more interesting and tangible so that students begin to care about the material.

Using real-life scenarios makes it easier for students to apply what they have learned in the classroom to the real world. They are not going to be able behave in the real world the same way they do in school; they may say something inappropriate or even playful to the wrong person. They will not have their teacher calling their parents on the phone explaining what they need to do to figure out such situations.

Self-efficacy is essential for the long-term success of students. To that end, adding real-life scenarios to the curriculum is paramount, because when the students behave at school more freely, without a sense of social norms or decorum, they are more likely to get into trouble with an individual or an institution. Thus, it is vital for them to learn SEL skills at school to avoid future problems.

REAL CLASSROOM EXAMPLES

A math or special education class provides an excellent example of where SEL-related activities can be used to enhance learning and engagement. The students can learn and use SEL skills and responsible decision-making during various activities:

As a warm-up, students can be called upon during "spin the wheel." They then approach the board and solve the problems on the board as the class observes. After the warm-up, the class works with the same partners during a challenge. The pairs of students are given cups with pennies in them. The teacher places a timer on the overhead projector and explains that the students are to stack as many pennies as they can, without touching the pennies, within the given time (one minute and thirty seconds). The teacher counts the pennies that each pair stacks, and the students record their data on a Post-It note. Students can assist each other during this activity, which helps greatly in accomplishing their tasks more easily and quickly.

This activity is extremely SEL focused because it incorporates a team collaboration effort, a range of social skills, and a responsible decision-making process. The students are highly engaged in the activity and are solution oriented. The competition with other teams also motivates them to succeed. The teacher facilitates their learning in two ways: updating students on the time remaining and providing reminders about the progress they should have made by that point.

Various social studies practices include discussions of old TV shows and themes, a life project that details a future budget and profession, and a war simulation. These class activities provide an opportunity to approach students with warmth while socially and emotionally engaging them at some level.

Consider this example of how one US history teacher taught social awareness and social intelligence. The teacher asked students to look for various themes in 1950s sitcoms, including fear, the family unit, differences between good and evil, and the return of innocence. He showed the class clips of TV shows and asked them which theme corresponded with which sitcom. The teacher demonstrated emotional intelligence to his students when he asked them to share their ideas and opinions as he called on specific students in a jovial manner that encouraged participation.

The teacher mostly ignored poor behavioral choices that negatively impacted student learning. The collaborative aspect of this activity was a class discussion. He related to students when he asked if they had seen a TV show called *The Killing*, a show his wife was watching at the time. While probing the students, he asked them, "What do you see?" Comparing the current broadcasting policies with older ones, he taught them that it is illegal to advertise smoking now—which the TV show *Father Knows Best* did in its opening credits.

He then showed students a Thanksgiving scene from *Father Knows Best* and stated that the message portrayed in the sitcom was not one that would typically be seen in a modern sitcom. He paused frequently to teach and talk. He asked the class, "Do girls usually cook and serve now?" His commentary during the videos was suspenseful and engaging.

The teacher kept predictors of success on the board—including grit, gratitude, self-control, optimism, social intelligence, conscientiousness, and curiosity—and there were checkmarks below each predictor, prompting students to select "best," "okay," or "lacking" to observe whether they were proficient with these skills. Students recorded the theme each sitcom represented. The class structure was exceptional at cultivating a positive socioemotional student environment where students could thrive in the subject matter. The teacher's ability to ignore minor misbehaviors helped maintain the class learning flow and left him in a positive mood.

During an economics class, the SEL focus can be responsible decision-making. Students may be assigned a project called "The Project of My Life," where they explore their prospective career, budget, the type of house they could buy, free time, and amortization rate. The project's purpose is to inform and prepare the students for the future. During such a project, students are expected to learn how the decisions they make today could significantly impact their future.

Traditional classrooms rely on individual work, but there are ways to conduct group collaboration and student-to-student interaction to advance SEL. Student learning occurs more frequently during student-to-student interactions. Student can collaborate to brainstorm certain aspects of a project and share their findings in a presentation where they interact with the class. Presentations can include student-led discussions, questions, and student-created games.

Over the last ten years, students' treatment of one another has improved. They have gradually become kinder and more tolerant. In some ways this contradicts the current tensions and the uncertainty in the political world. A simulation of World War I in history class can be an effective tool to capture these differences. The teacher can request that classes keep the peace while advancing the interests of their own country. Students negotiate, give up territory and claims, and learn to share their land and resources with their peers.

Gradually, through trial and error, the students came up with ways they could all live together. The teacher believed this reaction was indicative of what students expected from their adults, considering the real-life strife facing their society. The students needed a level of stability that they could not see in the outside world. This class was a hallmark class for SEL at the school because productive student-to-student interactions occurred during class discussions, war simulations, and more.

TAKEAWAYS FOR STUDENT RESPONSIBLE DECISION-MAKING

Students look up to their teachers for modeling. Teachers can lead by example with self-control. Showing students that the teacher cares will motivate them to learn the content. Furthermore, creating the rules together at the beginning of the year encourages student ownership. This is particularly effective when holding students accountable to the rules, because they created them. Asking the students to enforce the rules will more likely ensure their compliance with the rules.

The use of SEL can enhance content instruction. SEL can be infused into everyday practices by sharing interesting facts related to the content. It is important to take the time to get to know students' interests so that lessons and activities can be adjusted accordingly. Using real-life scenarios to connect content instruction makes the content more tangible and relatable. Adding humor helps keep everything lighthearted and fun, making it easier to teach and to learn.

Team collaboration can be used to the teacher's advantage. Student learning occurs mostly during student-to-student interactions. They learn from student-led instruction such as presentations, student-led discussions, debates, and games. They become the leaders of their own learning and take the pressure off the teacher.

QUESTIONS FOR REFLECTION

1. How can the use of real-life scenarios encourage students' responsible decision-making?
2. How can educators use questions and discussions about what is occurring outside the classroom to promote students' responsible decision-making?
3. How can group work be used to foster students' responsible decision-making?

ANSWERS TO QUESTIONS FOR REFLECTION

Teachers can use circle time, discussions, role-plays, and debates to encourage students' responsible decision-making. They can also use questions and discussions to promote responsible decision-making by meeting students at their level. Educators should discuss with students what good decision-making looks like. Group work can foster responsible decision-making because collaboration forces students to learn how to make decisions effectively within a group to meet requirements within a deadline.

REFERENCES

Dahlgren, Rick, and Judy Hyatt. 2007. *Time to Teach: Encouragement, Empowerment, and Excellence in Every Classroom with Refocus.* Hayden Lake, ID: Center for Teacher Effectiveness.

PART IV

Supporting Relationship Skills for Educators and Students

Chapter 7

Encouraging Relationship Skills for Educators

When educators treat their students with respect, the students feel a strong relationship and connection, even when studying subject areas many resist, such as math or science. This ability of teachers to foster strong connections with their students within a difficult subject matter indicates that SEL inclusion is possible across all subject areas. More importantly, it is even more necessary for those challenging subjects. Unless they feel supported, students simply do not learn as well or as much.

A TOUGH JOB MADE EASIER

There exists a dichotomy at school: Teachers must balance academic content and everyday life skills. Everything that is performed in the classroom is in the context of the subject matter. Teachers can keep lessons fresh by finding experiments and demonstrations that allow students to "see the subject matter in action" and apply their critical-thinking skills. If the teacher simply reiterates the content without connecting to the students, they learn the content without context. The teacher and the students will burn out quickly. The students will not like the teacher, the teacher will not like the students, and the class will become meaningless.

Review is essential. For instance, when an educator initially provides context for a challenging chapter, most of the students will understand it. But if the educator does not continue to review the chapter with the students, over time the content becomes abstract and loses its meaning. As a result, students lose the meaning of the unit. They must practice the concepts multiple times to solidify them. They must return to concrete ideas after breaks. The goal should be to foster meaningful content, or at the very least to create concrete concepts for the students.

Overall, teaching SEL makes teaching easier, as SEL helps make the class well structured. The students should know where to retrieve all the assignments and references, which makes it easier for the students to decide what to do if they want to improve their grades. They can take ownership of their work, particularly in middle school and high school, so they know not to turn to the teacher with questions such as, "What can I do to raise my grade?" Educators enjoy giving students a little bit more responsibility through this consistent, reliable structure. Beyond the structure, it is relationship building that makes everything possible.

One possible activity to be performed every day is the "picture of the day." This is a classroom management tool where the educator shows a fascinating picture, sometimes from the teacher's life, sometimes from science, space, nature, or another interesting topic. This can help build common ground that the teacher and students both find interesting, simply because it goes beyond the content area. This simple gesture allows the class to run smoothly because it helps students relate to the teacher, who is no longer just a person who loves the content.

Sharing something about yourself as an educator is an excellent way to connect with students. This makes the students feel more comfortable sharing about themselves, which creates a positive learning environment. To explain difficult concepts, educators may connect the concept to their everyday lives by using examples from school or from their lives outside of school. Teachers can probe students to understand the concepts that emerge through the content, further engaging in their learning and meaning-making processes.

Whenever there is an opportunity during a class discussion to connect the content with a personal story, educators should do so. Educators can ask questions, elicit responses, and then collectively connect the students' responses to whatever they are studying. Initiating student responses through journal writing is particularly relevant in humanities or social studies classes.

Students can be very revealing about their personal lives and dreams when they write, and so teachers feel compelled to support them more. Teachers can provide students with reflection activities to help them make connections between their own lives and the subject matter. These can include personal or academic reflections. At the beginning of students' senior year, they frequently write personal narratives, which can reveal and elucidate much of the students' background and struggles.

UNIQUE OPPORTUNITIES TO USE SEL AND RELATIONSHIP SKILLS

Educators are in a unique position to cultivate SEL skills in their students. It is important for teachers to clearly communicate behavioral and academic expectations to their students. They can also help resolve interpersonal conflicts and build meaningful relationships with colleagues and students (Yoder 2014).

ELA has an advantage over other subjects for SEL because of the tendency to be more revealing. In math, for instance, one does not write about one's life and obstacles. Other subject areas have different prompts. Students are naturally very revealing in ELA courses because they are often asked to use their personal history for assignments. Seniors also typically express these personal narratives during the college application process. When students write essays describing their obstacles and how they have overcome them, the social and emotional piece becomes clear.

There is a relational capacity between humanities instructors and their students that allows the social-emotional component to be prevalent. Student responses can often result in socioemotional support. Students know when a teacher is open to them and is willing to provide extra time and support. Although it is challenging to develop these positive relationships and to provide student support with the short amount of time that teachers have with students in class, they must try to carve out some extra time. This can be arranged by being available for students at lunch or after school.

Students are more likely to accomplish their tasks if they have support, both socioemotionally and academically. The extra time teachers provide students allows the content to become more tangible and relatable. Similarly, receiving teacher support helps students to mitigate negative situations at home that are out of their control. Educators' ability to provide this constant, open availability is vital for the students. They must know that their teachers are available for authentic, reliable support.

RELATIONSHIP BUILDING AND EMPATHY

There are two components of nonviolent communication that help in relationship building: expressing honestly and receiving empathetically (Rosenberg 2015). Expressing honestly is the ability to provide open dialogue and a safe environment to express emotions freely and openly. Receiving empathetically is the ability to receive feedback and listen to others without judgment.

There are four components to receiving empathetically: observing, feeling, needing, and requesting (Rosenberg 2015). These four components provide context for the process. For instance, individuals first observe their feelings, then allow themselves to feel them and decide on what they need. After that, they request what they need from others.

Empathy is understanding what others experience. It is possible only when we have removed all preconceived notions and judgments about others (Rosenberg 2015). Teachers should ask their students if they would like their advice or reassurance before providing it.

The more we empathize with others, the safer we feel. It is more difficult to demonstrate empathy for those who have power and prestige (Rosenberg 2015). It is natural for those who are lower in the hierarchy to hear commands and judgments from those who are above them. Therefore, it is helpful for educators to show empathy toward their administrators instead of passing judgment or becoming defensive or apologetic with them.

Empathy provides the ability to receive "no" without interpreting it as a rejection, revitalize a stagnant conversation, and understand feelings and needs even during silence (Rosenberg 2015). People can overcome issues more effectively when those who are listening to them are empathetic.

Positive connections require mutual trust, respect, and understanding (Hubble, Duncan, and Miller 1999). To maintain trust, we avoid people who make us feel uncomfortable. Students feel comfortable being vulnerable with adults they trust. For respect to occur, educators must also respect their students. People gravitate to those who show positive regard and make them feel valued. Educators should provide interest and optimism to the classroom environment to receive their students' respect. Lastly, understanding refers to empathy. Students connect with adults who show empathy to their needs.

Students do not respond well to negativity such as commands, distant tones, and avoidance. Kids innately understand cues that indicate teachers are disengaged and disinterested in them. They will demonstrate the same disinterest, disrespect, and negativity toward teachers who demonstrate this behavior. It is important as educators to keep a positive outlook every day, no matter what is going on in their lives. This is not easy, but students have more respect toward the teachers who share stories about their personal lives and show vulnerability. Students will view likeable teachers as deserving their empathy in return.

Students respond in two different ways in crisis: Either they isolate themselves in contemplation or they seek out the guidance from a trusted adult (Hubble, Duncan, and Miller 1999). It is a misconception that ignoring negative behavior in the classroom is always the answer. Students who are acting out may need an adult to listen to their issues for the behavior to stop. When educators provide support in times of crisis, misbehaving students feel stronger bonds with them.

There are simple ways to address students who are distant and difficult to reach. Teachers can use small interactions to increase trust. They do not need to rush a relationship with these students. One of the best ways to connect with them is to find their strengths and interests. It is vital to listen to students but not provide advice unless it is upon their request. Students do not appreciate embarrassing comments or insults.

POSITIVE FRAMING

Teachers should have a positive demeanor that provides hope to students. Students value transparency in building a relationship. It works best when teachers show that they enjoy spending time around young people, which can be accomplished through respecting them and giving them power.

For positive framing to occur, teachers can guide students to improve upon their work by using a positive tone and delivering constructive feedback. This will motivate and inspire students to continue improving. Positive reinforcement should be deliberate and include recognition and approval (Lemov 2015). Celebrations of learning are enjoyable ways to motivate students even more.

Teachers can simultaneously be both friendly and strict, delivering high expectations while being caring and respectful. Those who manage their own emotions well are the most effective in helping student achievement (Lemov 2015).

Teachers can make corrections in positive ways, such as using humor, deflection, and exclamations. Students also enjoy being challenged. They excel at competition, either within their class or with other classes.

UNIQUE CHILD BEHAVIORS

The behavior in children that influences our relationships with them is most affected by genetics (Dick 2021). Educators cannot control the behaviors of children but can learn to deal with their individual needs.

Genetic disposition plays a large role in shaping child behavior. Twins who are genetically identical share 50 percent of the same genes (Dick 2021). Studies have shown that identical twins raised by different families have just as many similarities as those who are raised by the same family.

The way our brains are wired contributes to our mental tendencies toward fear, anxiety, frustration, and reward seeking. Our brain patterns also influence our attention, memory, and thinking, as well as the ways we best learn.

Our temperament and appearance influence our experience in the world. We interpret and react to the world differently based on our genetics. Even children growing up in the same family can have very different experiences with their parents because of their unique genetic dispositions. Our genotypes influence the environments we seek out. Highly extroverted children, for example, seek out environments with a lot of people.

What works for one child may not work for another because children respond to the adults in their lives and environments in different ways. We can work with children's genetic dispositions to help them better navigate the world. Our own dispositions—or our three E's: extraversion, emotionality, and effortful control—explain much about our behaviors and personalities (Dick 2021). They can help both parents and educators determine their own personalities and the way they interact with their children and students.

Instead of discipline, educators can reward students for positive behavior using sticker charts, praises, treats, and the like. Using a mix of activities can help both introverted and extroverted students. When teachers use a combination of talking activities and individual work, accompanied by a routine of rewarding good behavior, consequences are needed far less frequently. Using positive language and stating the positive behaviors expected is promoted in PBIS (Dick 2021).

Time-outs are a classic consequence that can actually serve as a reward and not necessarily as a punishment (Dick 2021). A time-out could be a necessary brain break from a difficult task. No consequences should be given when the educator is angry. Educators should ignore bad behavior and attend to good behavior. High-emotionality students have more outbursts, tantrums, and behavioral issues, but it is important to remember that they did not choose to be this way. This understanding helps educators react appropriately to such student behavior.

TAKEAWAYS FOR EDUCATOR RELATIONSHIP SKILLS

It is important to build a collaborative relationship with students (Dick 2021). Find out what their triggers for outbursts are and transition between activities. Challenges occur for high-emotionality students when someone is unavailable, when there is a change in plans, or when things do not turn out as hoped. Keeping a journal on a particular child in question can be insightful for future interactions. Children are often dealing with overwhelming emotions that they do not know how to manage, and teachers may not know how to manage such students until they reflect on the behavior notes and consider a plan of action.

Teachers play many different roles including but not limited to the following: nurse, mentor, social worker, therapist, parent, cheerleader, tutor, and college adviser (Feldman 2019). Teachers enjoy working with children and often perform all these roles for their students. There may come a point when teachers need to create boundaries to protect themselves from overwork and burnout. It is not humanly possible for one person to always serve in these roles without personal repercussions.

Teachers should respect their students. It is difficult to balance SEL and content knowledge, but when they are balanced, the rewards are astounding. Using SEL in the classroom aids in avoiding burnout. Not all students will enjoy the content area, but they will enjoy getting to know their teachers and their classmates. Everyone needs human connection. Teachers can use this need to their advantage when teaching content to the students.

Classes need to be well structured and connected with personal stories. Students need reflection activities. They need to know that the teacher is there for support. When teachers show empathy toward their school's administration, students will feel better because it sets an example for them to be empathetic toward everyone, regardless of their position in the hierarchy. An administrator's job is a difficult one, too, and it can involve a lot of discipline, which teachers often perceive as a negative aspect of teaching.

Teachers must respect the students to receive their respect in return. Small interactions can increase trust. Rewarding students for positive behaviors is one way to do this. Avoiding negativity is essential for successful relationships with colleagues and students.

QUESTIONS FOR REFLECTION

1. How can educators share about themselves in a way that they feel comfortable to improve the student-teacher relationship?
2. How can teachers keep everything positive and avoid the negativity that may disrupt learning?
3. How can teachers strike a healthy balance between being too firm and too friendly?

ANSWERS TO QUESTIONS FOR REFLECTION

Teachers can share about themselves in ways that are appropriate and relevant to the school environment. This information can be about their families, weekend activities, and hobbies. When teachers are open about themselves, their students feel more comfortable sharing their own experiences. This open environment makes it easier for students to learn and for teachers to teach. Open dialogue can occur in any course subject. In some contexts it is necessary to address negative topics, but where it is not, teachers can and should avoid difficult and/or negative topics.

It is essential that teachers strike a balance between appearing as a friend and as a strict authority figure. When educators present themselves as too friendly with their students, they are taken advantage of; likewise, when educators are too rigid, students are less likely to be interested in the educator's contribution to the learning process. Firmness is the best portrayal, where educators are respected and students still feel comfortable approaching them with issues that must be addressed.

REFERENCES

Dick, Danielle M. 2021. *The Child Code: Understanding Your Child's Unique Nature for Happier, More Effective Parenting*. New York: Avery.

Feldman, Joe. 2019. *Grading for Equity: What It Is, Why It Matters, and How It Can Transform Schools and Classrooms*. Thousand Oaks, CA: Corwin.

Hubble, Mark A., Barry L. Duncan, and Scott D. Miller. 1999. *The Heart and Soul of Change: What Works in Therapy*. Washington, DC: American Psychological Association.

Lemov, Doug. 2015. *Teach Like a Champion 2.0: 62 Techniques That Put Students on the Path to College*. San Francisco: Joseey-Bass.

Rosenberg, Marshall B. 2015. *Nonviolent Communication: A Language of Life*. Encinitas, CA: PuddleDancer Press.

Yoder, Nicholas. 2014. *Self-Assessing Social and Emotional Instruction and Competencies: A Tool for Teachers*. Washington, DC: American Institutes for Research. Retrieved from https://files.eric.ed.gov/fulltext/ED553369.pdf.

Chapter 8

Encouraging Relationship Skills for Students

The quality of teacher-student relationships has been repeatedly linked with students' academic, social, and emotional outcomes. The good news is that, as an educator, you can design and implement practices that support this growth. If you want students to show initiative, create opportunities for them to make choices about how they learn (Martinez Perez 2020).

Turnover is exceptionally high at schools in neighborhoods with low socio-economic status due to the burnout that can result from working with students who live in poverty (Martinez Perez 2020). This is where the teacher-student relationship has been broken. In such situations, teachers can do activities that take a lesser toll on themselves, ensuring that they find purpose and joy in working with their students. The well-being of the teacher is almost a prerequisite to developing resilience in students.

Teachers have a key role in supporting students who have been exposed to trauma and diversity. As an educator, you can become a protective factor. When we are scared, our amygdala activates, sending emergency signals to our brain and body so we can protect ourselves from danger. Therefore, it is important to create a safe space in the classroom and use self-care strategies that will help support your energy and commitment to the work.

Prolonged stressful situations impair our ability to learn and maintain physical health. Schools and classroom teachers must prioritize on creating a sense of belonging for students that encouraged strong bonds (Martinez Perez 2020). Increasing the learning capacity of students involves having high expectations for their learning and developing their academic mindsets.

Educators should develop student-centered instruction where students are actively responsible and engaged, allowing them to take ownership in their own learning. When students develop these mindsets, their self-concept and sense of affiliation to the school are increased. To facilitate this, educators can provide feedback on effort and process.

THE NEED FOR CONNECTION AND CULTURE

Students need meaningful connections with adults to feel cared for and be motivated to learn. When fostering these connections, educators must keep in mind that students develop social, emotional, and academic skills at different rates. Educators can foster relationship skills in their students by creating shared ownership through honoring one's emotions and applying empathy (Martinez Perez 2020).

Culture is central to student learning because cultural practices shape the students' thinking process. Culturally responsive educators respect the languages, cultures, and life experiences of their students. What can educators learn about their students' languages, cultures, and life experiences that can help them better serve their students? Surveys and class discussions that occur in a safe classroom environment with a positive culture can provide valuable information for the educators regarding this.

Currently 34.8 million children—half the child population of the United States—are affected by adverse childhood experiences (ACEs; Martinez Perez 2020). These students experience toxic stress, rejection, low self-worth, and a lack of trust toward their teachers.

When the toxic stress students experience is not treated, they may have health concerns and develop mental health issues such as depression, anxiety, substance abuse, or suicide. Children with ACEs often develop learning disabilities and have difficulties with attention, concentration, memory, and creativity (Martinez Perez 2020). Therefore, it is essential for educators to foster a greater sense of belonging in the classroom.

COLLABORATION TOOLS AND CONFLICT RESOLUTION

Students typically work best in small groups of not more than two to four; larger groups make it challenging for everyone to participate effectively in the group. For some activities it is better to let the students work together most of the time, jumping in only when interaction is needed. Students gradually learn from each other about how to interact within their peer groups, so by the age of fifteen, many students are already proficient with interaction skills. The teacher's role, then, should be to improve this natural tendency toward interaction, fostering effective collaboration and team-building skills.

The tools for collaboration are learned beginning in early childhood and are commonly called "getting along with others" by children. A well-collaborating child can join a group of other children without causing meltdowns or tantrums (Bilmes 2012). A child who is poor at collaborating will constantly have disputes with others because they lack the foundation necessary for friendship skills.

Punishing children does not help them develop the skills they need to thrive when they are older. Punishment and other negative and hurtful strategies are fruitless. Instead, educators should focus efforts on building relationship skills with children and assist them in developing friendship skills (Bilmes 2012).

Consider the following reflection questions when ensuring the development of students' relationship skills: Twenty years from now, what kind of personal qualities would you like to see in your students? What strengths are your students developing? What can you do to encourage them to develop those strengths? (Bilmes 2012)

Collaboration occurs when a child learns how to understand the needs of other children and to negotiate constructively within the constraints of social rules and values. Children need to learn conflict-resolution and problem-solving skills (e.g., losing a personal item, being overwhelmed, feeling tired). The following interaction steps support conflict resolution for children:

1. Calming down
2. Talking about what they need and listening to what their peers need
3. Understanding the conflict
4. Thinking about and trying ways to solve the conflict
5. Going back to resolve the conflict if the first solution does not work (Bilmes, 2012)

In addition to these interactions, teachers can use the following questions to help children resolve conflicts on their own:

- What are you going to do?
- What are some ideas you have?
- How could you solve the conflict?
- What could you do now that is helpful?
- What could you do to resolve your conflict? (Bilmes, 2012)

Educators can help children express their needs and wants while demonstrating attitudes effective in conflict resolution. Conflicts can be resolved; nobody is all wrong or all right. The goal is to figure out what will happen next instead of assigning responsibility for what has already happened. A conflict is solved only when the solution works for everyone (Bilmes 2012).

Educators can help children see problems as temporary. The adults can teach children techniques such as imagining telling off the people who have wronged them so they can release the tension in their mind. If you imagine it is, of course, not the same as telling someone off. Other coping strategies include restoring oneself by hugging someone they trust to release oxytocin (Van Susteren and Colino 2020).

There are multiple influential ways to make a positive difference in the lives of the troubled youth. Educators should treat all students the same, without favoritism. However, classroom discipline requires keeping emotional distance from the students. It is important to not let children become dependent upon the educator. Educators who become emotionally involved may experience burnout (Brendtro and du Toit 2005). Close relationships may also place the educator at risk for accusations of sexual abuse.

Students are less likely to be academically prepared if they have recently experienced trauma. One way to mitigate trauma is through teamwork and collaboration. When students work together as equals to achieve a common goal, such as on a team or in a classroom, stereotypes break down and they start to work together as a community (Goleman 2005).

An attachment is any close, ongoing relationship the child has with one or more adults inside or outside of the home. Attachments have these characteristics: looking to them for love and affection; depending upon them for safety and security; counting on them for knowledge, wisdom, and guidance; and accepting their help and comfort. A child who does not have an attachment to a teacher or a caring family member may flinch or look away. Sometimes, differences between the teacher's and the family's expectations about how to interact with adults in authority can result in problems between teacher and child (Bilmes 2012).

SUPPORTIVE RELATIONSHIP BUILDING

Supportive interactions to promote attachment include getting to know children well, interacting with affection, and recognizing feelings (Bilmes 2012). Direct interactions, especially with younger children, is the best way to help develop language skills. Educators should not compliment outward appearances, instead saying things like, "I'm happy to see you," "I'm happy when I see your smile," or "Tell me about your recent visit with a family member."

Educators should focus on the need for safety when disciplining children. Direct communication style can help ensure that students do not misinterpret what the adults say (Bilmes 2012). Using the word "come" instead of the command "go"—for instance, "Come, let's wash your hands" instead of "Go wash your hands"—is more polite and welcoming, and the child is more likely to respond positively to this approach.

When an educator must be absent, writing a note to students about the need for a substitute that day and how they can do their work can calm their fears about sudden change. For younger students, the note can be displayed in case they need to refer to it later.

All children require at least one caring adult in their lives, but many troubled kids do not have one (Brendtro and du Toit 2005). These children project all their past trauma onto adults who are trying to positively impact their lives and do not trust the well-meaning adults. On the other hand, children who are emotionally healthy feel well connected at home and at school. Many of the problems in childhood are due to the "diagnosis of disconnection" (Hallowell 2002). This diagnosis of disconnection or the lack of human connection becomes a serious issue for students who do not have at least one caring adult in their lives.

When teachers succeed in gaining the trust of troubled students, they can redirect these students in any way they choose best for them. These children are in pain and need positive adult support to get through it. The boundaries these kids create are a method to detach and keep their feelings safe and guarded (Brendtro and du Toit 2005). All young people must be touched by acts of kindness that demonstrate they are valued.

BUILDING FRIENDSHIP SKILLS

For those students who do not have the friendship skills necessary to be successful, there are programs available to address the development of these skills in collaboration with educators and parents. One such program is the Program for the Education and Enrichment of Relational Skills (PEERS), an intervention on social skills for teens and young adults.

PEERS is a research platform that describes rules and steps in social behavior (Laugeson 2013). It is typically facilitated by mental health professionals and educators. Their goal is to teach friendship skills using parent-supported coaching.

Being social and making friends is an art. Decoding social behaviors into concrete rules and steps helps demystify the social world for the students. Teens and young adults with autism spectrum disorder (ASD), attention deficit hyperactivity disorder (ADHD), or other disorders often have difficulty maintaining friendships (Laugeson 2013). When parents and teachers have research-based and child-approved strategies to address ADHD, they are better equipped to help their children and students learn (Biscotti 2021). The key for such learners is to obtain their buy-in with learning and activities.

When students clearly understand learning objectives, they are better equipped to pay attention and stay focused. They also need to be on board with learning the objectives for the day. When they understand the rationale for learning that day, they are more likely to participate. Students with ADHD need clear expectations and structure to thrive. When they do not have this consistency, their ability to concentrate decreases.

Behavior plans between parents and teachers help keep students on track with learning objectives, especially in the early grades. When students have someone to regularly check in with, they are better able to prevent and address issues with deadlines as they arise.

Students with ADHD need support in setting goals, and they need to hear positive reinforcement for behaviors that are helpful in the classroom. They also need help with prioritization and pacing themselves. When they have a teacher and/or parent advocating for them to ensure that these needs are met, they are better able to thrive. Thankfully, these skills are helpful for all students, with and without ADHD. Procrastination, concentration, and motivation can be issues for all learning types.

Social groups provide protection from individual bullying and victimization (Laugeson 2013). Such groups are needed to find a potential source of friends and to feel connected to something larger than oneself, which are important parts of adolescence and adulthood.

Although finding the right social group is a personal choice and will vary according to interests and hobbies, it is also important to understand the cultural meaning and evolving characteristics of social groups. Characteristics of good friendships include sharing of common interests, caring, support, mutual understanding, commitment, loyalty, honesty, trust, equality, ability to self-disclose, and conflict resolution (Laugeson 2013).

TAKEAWAYS FOR STUDENT RELATIONSHIP SKILLS

Teachers who use emotional intelligence and social emotional learning in their classrooms insist that their students advocate for themselves in a positive way, learn in a positive environment, and support each other in academic work. Specifically, it is essential to help students to discover their voice so that they can "unlock their power." The results suggest that student buy-in improves academic achievement. Students tend to reveal more of their personal lives in ELA classes. This gives an advantage to ELA teachers over other subject area teachers regarding teaching SEL.

The result is that more humanities teachers are willing to teach SEL because they see its direct impact and benefit. It is much more feasible for them to authentically incorporate SEL competencies into their curriculum.

Moreover, teaching SEL also makes other subject areas, such as math, easier to teach, especially when students are motivated to take ownership of their work and learning. This means that math and science teachers should not give up on teaching SEL. Even though it is more challenging to teach SEL in these subject areas, the outcome is more rewarding.

Knowledge of student profiles helps teachers to plan lessons and remediate when there are unexpected learning challenges. Goleman (2005) suggests blending lessons on feelings and relationships with academic topics.

One way to build relationships is to decorate the classroom to be more comfortable and "homier" to motivate students. In other words, teachers who take the initiative to comfort students are more likely to have students who are more motivated in their content areas. This initiative also solidifies relationships between teachers and students.

Students should be encouraged to do group work so that they can practice their collaboration skills. They also need conflict-resolution competencies to readily resolve problems with their peers on their own. When students are dealing with trauma, conflicts tend to escalate. Teachers can encourage counselor teaching sessions of life skills and practicing complimenting one another to foster positive peer relationships within students. Interactive activities that allow students to perform skits, role-play, debate, and participate in other activities are exciting ways for them to improve relationships with peers.

When students are encouraged to unlock their own power and voice, they can positively communicate their needs and desires to their peers. This open communication allows for a positive learning environment with a give-and-take approach to student learning. Students learn to directly provide one another with the social and emotional support when it is role modeled by adults such as teachers and counselors.

Teacher-student relationships are interconnected with social-emotional and academic outcomes. Teachers can find purpose and joy in their work to avoid burnout, which will allow them to better serve their students. Educators can become a protective factor for students who have been exposed to trauma and diversity.

Culturally responsive teachers respect students' language, culture, and life experiences. Teachers can foster a sense of belonging. When the toxic stress experiences are not treated, they may develop into other health concerns such as depression, anxiety, and substance abuse. Children with ACEs can develop disabilities and difficulties with attention, concentration, memory, and creativity. These students experience toxic stress rejection and low self-worth.

It is essential to assist the children with deficiencies in friendship skills and the ability to collaborate. By age fifteen, many students are already proficient in interaction skills. Punishment can do more damage than benefit.

Collaboration occurs when children can empathize with and understand the needs of other children. Conflict resolution is essential for positive relationships to occur, and a conflict is resolved only when it works for everyone.

It is important to treat all students equally and not provide preferential treatment. It is also necessary to not become emotionally involved, which can be exhausting. Encouraging students to work together as a community will help them build rapport and culture. Teaching students to advocate for themselves in positive ways will alleviate future conflicts. Students can be encouraged to resolve issues independently with others before asking the educator for guidance.

QUESTIONS FOR REFLECTION

1. How can educators prevent students from becoming too dependent upon them?
2. How can educators not become too emotionally involved with student traumas?
3. How can educators help their students unlock their power/voice?

ANSWERS TO REFLECTION QUESTIONS

Educators can prevent students from becoming too dependent upon them by encouraging them to ask a peer first when they do not know the answer. Educators can also allow students to speak in low voices, to collaborate, and to do group work when appropriate. Collaboration is a method that can help students foster their own problem-solving skills without relying on the teacher.

To avoid emotional involvement with students, educators can distance their own emotions from the difficult problems of their students, whether it is homelessness, losing a family member, or a parent losing their job. The ability to distance emotions is no easy feat, but it can occur through regular reflection, journaling, and meditation/prayer. When we jot down thoughts that are troubling us, we are better able to release them.

Another approach to avoiding traumatic conversations is to tell the student experiencing trauma that unfortunately, you cannot hear more because you are a mandated reporter for Child Protective Services (CPS). You can recommend that the student speak to a counselor, but you do not want to be placed in a situation where you are obligated to contact CPS out of fear of losing your job.

Teachers can aid their students in unlocking their power and voice by providing assignment choices. Students can find their voices not only orally but also in written assignments. They are more likely to feel empowered when writing about their personal experiences. After further reflection and when they feel they are in a safe place, they may be more likely to share their personal experiences with the class. These share-outs can create an even safer environment for other students to feel emboldened enough to share out and find their voice.

REFERENCES

Bilmes, Jenna. 2012. *Beyond Behavior Management: The Six Life Skills Children Need.* 2nd ed. St. Paul, MN: Redleaf Press.

Biscotti, Nicole. 2021. *I Can Learn When I'm Moving: Going to School with ADHD.* Quincy, MA: EduMarch.

Brendtro, Larry, and Lesley du Toit. 2005. *Response Ability Pathways: Restoring Bonds of Respect.* Cape Town, South Africa: Pretext.

Goleman, Daniel. 2005. *Emotional Intelligence.* New York: Bantam.

Hallowell, . 2002. *Connections.* Paper presented at the National Adolescent Conference, Scottsdale, AZ.

Laugeson, Elizabeth A. 2013. *The Science of Making Friends: Helping Socially Challenged Teens and Young Adults.* San Francisco: Jossey-Bass.

Martinez Perez, Lorea. 2020. *Teaching with the Heart in Mind: A Complete Educator's Guide to Social Emotional Learning.* New York: Brisca Publishing.

Van Susteren, Lisa, and Stacey Colino. 2020. *Emotional Inflammation: Discover Your Triggers and Reclaim Your Equilibrium during Anxious Times.* Louisville, CO: Sounds True.

PART V

Encouraging Social Awareness for Educators and Students

Chapter 9

Developing Social Awareness for Educators

According to Duckworth and Seligman (2005), people who describe their experience in pessimistic ways have a higher risk of depression, lower academic and professional achievement, and lower-quality physical health than those who hold optimistic views.

Students are more willing to perform well if they know there are adults at the school who wish them well. Such actions as administrators visiting parents' workplaces to discuss behavioral issues at school are effective ways to foster family-home connections that promote social-emotional learning.

By conducting home visits, educators communicate that they care on a deeper level and are willing to go beyond the job description and do what is best for students. Teachers increasingly are trying to understand where their students are coming from, and they truly want their students to be successful.

BECOMING SOCIALLY AWARE EDUCATORS

A culture and climate team can focus on responding to misbehaviors. The team can outline a range of misbehaviors and categorize them by the level of offense, adopt a list of misbehaviors, collaborate on how best to respond to various types of offenses, and use SEL program materials as a resource.

Educators may feel guilty about stopping instruction to deal with social-emotional issues because they are concerned about falling behind in content (Martinez Perez 2020). Including SEL in every lesson can ease the process of dealing with social-emotional issues, particularly trauma, when they do arise. When we honor our emotions, we can use emotional words to describe our feelings. We can reflect on them and use these words to communicate our emotions to others.

The beginning of a lesson is an important time to create interest and stimulate curiosity (Martinez Perez 2020). Successful educators use tools at the beginning of their lessons to hook the attention of their students for the rest of the lesson. Such tools include short videos, compelling stories, thought-provoking questions, and enticing visuals.

SEL makes it easier to teach any subject area. For instance, in physics, it is effective to bridge the content with something students care about and are interested in knowing more about. If the students are engaged and interested, and can connect with the content, they begin to realize that the content has an application in the future that goes beyond the next assignment or the next test. In this way, it is easier for a teacher to drive content forward.

When educators understand students' perspectives and pay attention to their emotional, verbal, and physical cues during classroom interactions, they are better able to address the students' needs. When students are not interacting or as engaged as expected, educators can try to understand why. They can support positive interactions and respond appropriately to negative emotions. Furthermore, educators can address commonalities and differences that exist among students in productive ways (Yoder 2014).

THE POLITICAL NATURE OF TEACHING IN TODAY'S WORLD

Teaching has become very political due to climate change, reproductive rights, gun violence, civil unrest, war, critical race theory, and more. Teachers recognize that it is not feasible to meet all the political and standardized testing requirements within the required timeframe.

There is simply not enough instruction time to address the curriculum pacing guides and the content on standardized tests mandated by the school districts. Educators must prioritize. If required to submit lesson plans ahead of time, teachers would be limited to addressing large-scale national and international events, which stifles social-emotional development. This restriction of teachers' ability to teach freely, speak freely, and teach their content without the pressure of standardized testing has become isolating and demeaning.

Keeping all the political changes in context, what are some ways in which educators can ignore the political backlash? Educators need to keep in mind that society is aware of their intelligence and influence over young minds. They can take this constant interfering with their curriculum and teaching as a compliment. They are being forced to reckon with societal inadequacies through no fault of their own, but due to their own desire to help develop productive citizens.

TAKEAWAYS FOR EDUCATOR SOCIAL AWARENESS

A constant connection to real life allows educators to ask more interesting questions that expand their thinking. This makes better teachers because those with a stagnant mindset are less likely to inspire interest in their students. Teachers' dedication to improve their own subject content knowledge over time suggests that they are invested in continued learning and growth for the sake of their students. Once a teacher stops caring about consistently updating their knowledge, it is no longer possible to effectively teach and engage students.

The purpose of teaching SEL in schools is to help students care more about their education so that they become successful and productive citizens. Currently, many students do not feel their schools care about them or are engaged enough in their learning. Thus, educators can incorporate SEL practices into their teaching to restore the faith and trust of their students.

Everyone can use words to label our emotions, and by doing that we honor their existence. Educators can use enticing videos, compelling questions, and powerful visuals to engage a class. Engaging a class is vital in making connections with students and building social-emotional connections among peers.

Questions for Reflection

1. How can teachers stay excited about learning so that they can teach enthusiastically and effectively?
2. How can a school create an SEL committee or a similar entity to best serve the community?
3. How can both teachers and students stay engaged in the content while socially-emotionally developing awareness?

ANSWERS TO QUESTIONS FOR REFLECTION

Attending conferences and professional development opportunities can help teachers remain excited about learning, which in turn enables them to teach enthusiastically and effectively. Conferences can introduce teachers to new and innovative methods to approach subjects that are difficult to teach.

Conferences can also provide a way for educators to collaborate and reenergize their love for teaching. Another way educators can stay enthused about teaching is to collaborate with other educators in the building or within their school district. Educators can learn new activities and improved ways of communicating concepts through such collaborations.

Schools can create an SEL committee by looking to other schools that have already set up such committees. Since there are many SEL programs, educators can verify with their school district which SEL programs are approved and discuss which ones would be a good fit for an individual school's culture and needs.

Educators can stay engaged in the content while developing their own social awareness by seeking feedback from students after lessons through an anonymous survey. Paper-based surveys are the easiest to make anonymous because students are not required to write their names.

A survey can be done at the end of a unit, quarter, or year. Educators can inform their students that they will read each survey and consider the feedback to make further improvements. Questions could be focused on social awareness and content acquisition, including: Do you feel comfortable sharing about yourself in this class? Why or why not? What would make you feel more comfortable to share out in this class?

REFERENCES

Duckworth, Angela L., and Martin E. P. Seligman. 2005. "Self-discipline Outdoes IQ Predicting Academic Performance in Adolescents." *Psychological Science* 16, no. 12 (December): 939–44.

Martinez Perez, Lorea. 2020. *Teaching with the Heart in Mind: A Complete Educator's Guide to Social Emotional Learning.* New York: Brisca Publishing.

Yoder, Nicholas. 2014. *Self-Assessing Social and Emotional Instruction and Competencies: A Tool for Teachers.* Washington, DC: American Institutes for Research. Retrieved from https://files.eric.ed.gov/fulltext/ED553369.pdf.

Chapter 10

Developing Social Awareness for Students

The early childhood years are the most critical in establishing the neural connections that provide the foundation for emotional health and social skills such as language, reasoning, and problem solving. When students experience trauma or recurrent stress at a young age as a result of their living situation, it impacts their nervous system and their ability to regulate their emotions (Martinez Perez 2020).

The negative effects of stress can be buffered through supportive parenting, relationships, community, and school programs. Educators should ask themselves: Are students' social and emotional development being supported? Is their well-being prioritized? Embracing all emotions includes embracing the unpleasant ones to endure a sense of happiness and life satisfaction (Martinez Perez 2020).

Educators understand the kinds of emotions students experience in the classroom, how these emotions differ among students, and how they influence students' engagement and performance. Based on this knowledge, educators can create the social and emotional conditions for an SEL-filled classroom. They can do this by making sure that students are physically, emotionally, and intellectually safe; that they are engaged and motivated to learn; and that they have an appropriate level of support and sense of belonging (Martinez Perez 2020).

When we nurture our students, they grow emotionally. Students cannot focus academically if they are experiencing strong emotions or are constantly stressed. Given the time constraints and academic pressure teachers face, many struggle to find ways to incorporate SEL into their teaching (Martinez Perez 2020).

SOCIAL MEDIA AND STUDENT SOCIAL AWARENESS

Social media is a widely unpoliced area where students feel free to say and do whatever they like and live in a fantasy world where they often have no regard for others' needs and feelings. Bullying on social media has been a recurring problem because there have been relatively few repercussions, but students need to know that threats are taken seriously and so are harassment and bullying.

Unfortunately, cyberbullying has become a real problem at schools. Schools can make a concerted effort to reach all their students by providing a variety of programs and support. To this end, administrations have found means to addressing cyberbullying at various levels, such as creating TV programs and posters to spread awareness in every classroom.

One way a school can respond to cyberbullying is by creating a short video that includes advice, instructions, and guidance from individuals such as the counselors, principal, school resource officers, police chief, and superintendent. The purpose of the video could be to demonstrate the myth of anonymity on social media and the serious repercussions of cyberbullying.

The video can ask students to think about the impact of their actions on others. A poster that reiterates the main points of the video can be displayed in every classroom. The poster can ask students to contemplate whether their actions are inspiring, helpful, or kind. The intent of the message is to prevent them from posting negative content on social media, which can be detrimental for their own reputations.

SOCIOECONOMIC STATUS AND STUDENT SOCIAL AWARENESS

Many students from families of low socioeconomic status are highly empathetic because they have experienced loss, grief, death, and poverty. These students can have an inclusive culture because of these grave experiences. Students in these circumstances often use code-switching to feel a sense of belonging both at home and at school. They know that the language they use at home may not be the same language they use at school; therefore, code-switching has become a necessary function of these students' everyday lives.

Students often struggle with the conflict between their home culture, which has defined who they were, and their societal culture, which defines who they are as well as who they want to be. There needs to be an understanding that everyone is at school to learn, and everyone is there to be kind.

Nonetheless, the diversity of the school population creates a challenge for schools to be welcoming places where everyone feels comfortable. Students need schools where they know they will be accepted. They also need to feel comfortable dressing according to their gender identity without criticism from other students.

SEL PROGRAMS AND STUDENT SOCIAL AWARENESS

Various SEL programs, including Capturing Kids' Hearts and CharacterStrong, exist to generate a positive learning environment. These programs recommend greeting students at the door at the beginning of class and creating social contracts or classroom rules democratically with each class. Training in these programs is aimed at promoting relationships with students as a foundation of teaching.

The Capturing Kids' Hearts program instills in teachers an understanding of student experiences and challenges. It aims to aid students in acknowledging who their teachers are so they can understand them on a human level and feel more comfortable confiding in them.

CharacterStrong offers SEL curricula for grades K–12 and places an emphasis on explaining the purpose behind the work. Schools must have the staff on board before they can expect students to complete the tasks. This program includes Character Dares that ask students to reach out to five other individuals for feedback about their relationships. There is also a CharacterStrong Gym that provides compliment starters.

THE HOME-SCHOOL CONNECTION

There needs to be an exposure to affiliated family and community that fosters an increased value for positivity at schools. Students are more likely to take pride in their school when they have family and friends who attended the same school. Having guest speakers who are professionals in their content area and well known in the community also foster a sense of pride in the students. Guest speakers provide opportunities for role modeling, and students can learn from successful members of their community about potential careers and various pathways that would be otherwise unknown to them.

STAFF EFFECTS ON STUDENT SOCIAL AWARENESS

Staff meetings serve to analyze data and decide outcomes. One important data point to discuss is staff surveys where educators can examine the DNF (did not finish) rate in student performance reviews. Teachers need opportunities to discuss their concerns about student performance and dropout rates. They need to recognize which groups of students are really struggling as well as the suspension and disciplinary actions. Some of the responses may be disconcerting; these may show a general awareness of SEL because they clearly identify the students' SEL needs.

Staff can also discuss data from standardized tests such as the Smarter Balanced assessment to explore whether the students are meeting benchmarks and decide on next steps or protocols needed to intervene and bridge the gap. SEL assessment data or school culture and climate surveys can suggest areas for growth, such as weak connections to the school among students. The administration may determine SEL needs by using these and other data sources.

Schools can leverage culture and climate team meetings as opportunities to find alternative ways to address issues revealed through the data. For instance, if the data show that students feel unsafe in a certain way, the staff can address and rectify this by promoting student involvement in the solutions. If students feel disconnected, the staff should discuss ways to make them feel more connected; consequently, they can find resources and activities to promote positive change. At the beginning of the year, staff can wear SEL-focused T-shirts and have SEL banners around the school to model what student excellence looks like.

HEALTHY RELATIONSHIPS AND GRIT

To prepare kids to participate in relationships as healthy individuals, they need to be open and receptive rather than closed and reactive (Siegel and Payne Bryson 2012). They need positive reinforcement about their relationships. Improv and role-play are excellent ways to mimic and practice social relationships.

In *Grit*, Angela Duckworth (2016) anecdotally describes how individuals can give back to their communities through their grit. She provides an example of a young Cinnabon Vice President, Kat Cole, who was extremely gritty. She learned to persevere through the example of her single mother, who always found time to help others even though she worked three jobs. Kat became a waitress at Hooters at the age of eighteen. When the cooks quit their jobs unexpectedly, she went into the kitchen and cooked so she could still get tips and help others. She continued to do the same every time a manager or anyone else quit.

Kat took on any role that was available to her and within six months had worked every role at the restaurant. Because of her tenacity, she went on to do trainings and became the manager of multiple Hooters locations domestically and internationally. At the end of her time at the Hooters franchise, Cinnabon recruited her for the position of vice president. At Cinnabon she increased sales more quickly than they had in a decade, and within four years sales exceeded $1 billion.

The moral of the story is that if as educators we can instill the social awareness in our students to care about others' needs, they could become the next Kat, who puts other peoples' needs before their own. Kat's intent was not to become an executive but to make extra money and help others. She is a model for the Hobbesian philosophy because she was a student who became incredibly prepared for society—and succeeded.

Takeaways for Student Social Awareness

Educators have a unique opportunity to foster a sense of purpose and spark students' interests. Students may think that they have only a few opportunities to consider when it comes to their future. Teachers can help them discover new paths and possibilities that they would not otherwise see on their own.

Not everyone is going to be a Kat Cole, but educators can help students discover their potential by encouraging them to step up to help others, stay engaged, and be motivated. In recent years, grit has been touted as the single most important ingredient for success in education trends. More importantly, it is the social awareness of those around them that will inspire students to care about their communities, discover their own passions, help others, and succeed themselves.

The early years are critical for establishing connections. Trauma can derive from recurring stress. Therefore, creating a sense of belonging should be a priority schoolwide. Students need a welcoming place where they will be accepted for who they are. SEL programs can be used to build social awareness. When teachers expect their students to perform well, students will live up to those high expectations.

Staff should be active participants in various data points such as graduation rates, suspension rates, attendance rates, school climate and culture survey results, and more. Administrators can leverage staff meetings for alternative ways to impact data. Providing positive reinforcements is necessary for students. Positive role models foster a sense of purpose that sparks students' interests while helping them to discover their potential.

Questions for Reflection

1. How can educators emphasize the importance of kindness to others?
2. How can educators teach their students to put others' interests before their own?
3. What are ways educators could improve home-school connections?

ANSWERS TO QUESTIONS FOR REFLECTION

Educators can emphasize the importance of kindness to others by modeling kindness to their students and fellow colleagues. Showing empathy improves learning outcomes because students feel more connected to educators who empathize with their students.

Undoing selfishness does not mean thinking less of yourself, it means thinking of yourself less often. Educators can teach their students about the positive outcomes of putting others' interests before their own by placing their students' interests before their own. When teachers survey their students and tailor lessons accordingly, they can understand their students' needs and connect with them more effectively.

Educators can improve home-school connections by contacting parents when their child performs well on assessments, presentations, or assignments. The good news will improve the child's relationship with their parents and with their teacher. Home-school connections can also be improved by regular communication through newsletters, progress reports, and the availability of the teacher to connect with parents.

REFERENCES

Duckworth, Angela. 2016. *Grit: The Power of Passion and Perserverance*. New York: Scribner.

Martinez Perez, Lorea. 2020. *Teaching with the Heart in Mind: A Complete Educator's Guide to Social Emotional Learning*. New York: Brisca Publishing.

Siegel, Daniel J., and Tina Payne Bryson. 2012. *The Whole-Brain Child: 12 Revolutionary Strategies to Nurture Your Child's Developing Mind*. New York: Bantam.

PART VI

The Development of SEL Competencies for Educators and Students

Chapter 11

SEL Professional Learning Communities

THE PURPOSE OF AN SEL PROFESSIONAL LEARNING COMMUNITY

An SEL-focused professional learning community will encourage teachers to share best practices and resources with their colleagues. It is a natural fit for the lack of current SEL collaboration at schools. Teachers are more likely to listen to their fellow colleagues about topics that work well in the classroom. An SEL Professional Learning Community (PLC) encourages the usage of SEL in the classroom, as teachers receive direct support from each other.

The benefits of PLCs include improved communication, relationships, and overall school culture and climate (Siano 2018). PLCs improve communication among school staff. Educators and administrators can collaborate on problems that are difficult to solve individually. PLCs are collaborative, engage members in asking questions, and encourage shared leadership (Hilliard and Newsome 2013; Nelson, LeBard, and Waters 2010; Stoll et al. 2006).

As administrators and educators work together, they improve objectives, lessons, and instruction. When administrators support their educators in an open dialogue, the positive exchange of ideas reverberates across the school (McCarley, Peters, and Decman 2016). Likewise, when teachers have positive relationships with their administrators, they experience higher job satisfaction (Rafferty 2003), and PLCs can even reduce teacher absences (Harris and Jones 2010).

TEACHERS AS SEL LEARNERS AND LEADERS

When it comes to SEL, everyone is a learner, including teachers. SEL is not possible in a school if the teachers themselves are not SEL-focused. Teachers who develop social-emotional skills in their own daily habits and in their interactions with others are more likely to develop social-emotional skills in their students. When teachers are not SEL-focused, they can be a hindrance to their students' SEL learning process.

Before any school decides to engage in an SEL program, the administration needs to work toward the growth of their staff. There is no better way to do this than to garner buy-in from teachers who are already passionate about SEL. School leaders can survey their staff to see who is already practicing SEL in their classrooms. This can help them determine who is likely to help other educators begin practicing it in their classrooms. Administrators may discover that they have incredible talent already in-house.

Administrators can leverage their SEL subject matter experts and empower them to deliver workshops and trainings to overwhelmed staff who do not know where to start with SEL inclusion. Educators will be more supportive of SEL after they realize that they need to make only small instructional changes to include SEL.

STAFF SEL PROFESSIONAL DEVELOPMENT

Administrators should purchase an SEL program that is well-suited for their school. Some of these programs provide staff training to develop SEL skills for themselves and their students. School leaders can use these trainings in addition to an organic in-house SEL PLC or other SEL-like committee, where educators from the school can also become leaders.

The one-time training an SEL program delivers could serve as the kickoff session to promote staff awareness of the importance of first developing SEL competencies in themselves. After completing the staff training, the SEL PLC or SEL committee will have homegrown SEL teacher advocates who can serve as coaches to provide suggestions and trainings.

LEVERAGING A PLC FOR SEL PROMOTION

Teachers in a schoolwide SEL PLC who serve as coaches or mentors for other teachers new to SEL may also act as in-house consultants to promote SEL in the school community. Teachers know their school communities better than any outside SEL program. They can make appropriate suggestions for what works best in their school through announcements, social media, hall posters, and emails. This knowledge is priceless and should be sought out as soon as a change to the school culture and climate occurs.

Moreover, members of a lead SEL PLC school team can further support grade-level or content-specific PLCs. In the typical PLC model, educators seek to discuss what students should know or be able to do (learning standards), how they as educators know when students have mastered the content (assessments), which strategies to implement when students do not achieve mastery (interventions), and what kind of support to provide for those who do master the content (enrichment). In a PLC focused on SEL, a grade-level or content-focused team could shift their data from academics to an SEL metric.

Examples of SEL-related data points include attendance, SEL student survey data, SEL family survey data, student advisory panels, and family advisory panels. As the team analyzes these data, they can determine problem statements and then discuss potential root causes. From there, action planning to target specific causes can improve the SEL conditions of students and staff alike.

Connections can be made to PLCs with the purpose of improving outcomes for low-performing students. This can be done by tailoring strategies and tools for the appropriate grade level, content area, and teaching style. It is helpful to start small, with one to two strategies that will help build relationships in the school building, and then adding more strategies to build intellective capacity (Hammond 2014).

A simple approach is to observe current practices and/or student learning behaviors to gain an understanding of the baseline (Hammond 2014). Regular data collection is necessary, for this is a research-based approach. Reflections and adjustments during data collection will better inform practices. Within a PLC, it is easy to foster individual and group collaboration and accountability regarding teachers' research-based approaches. It is important to make connections within the PLC throughout this action research. This collective research will initiate necessary change and hold all members of the PLC accountable for achieving the desired change.

The goal of the SEL-focused PLC is to build relationships with students and foster a social-emotional connection to provide a safe space for learning in the entire school building. Educators can collectively make student voice and agency a priority. Furthermore, they can build classroom culture and learning with communal talk and task structures. Classroom rituals and routines support the culture of learning, while restorative justice principles can mitigate conflicts and redirect negative behaviors (Hammond 2014).

DEVELOPING COMMUNITY

A homegrown SEL-focused community where the staff is willing to develop SEL in their students is the best. Teachers need to feel comfortable with the content and with the program chosen by school leaders. Educators who do not know the content will not feel comfortable delivering it. Educators need professional development to feel adequate at delivering SEL instruction both in their own content areas and with a designated SEL program that may be delivered in a homeroom-like course.

REFERENCES

Hammond, Zaretta L. 2014. *Culturally Responsive Teaching and the Brain: Promoting Authentic Engagement and Rigor among Culturally and Linguistically Diverse Students*. Thousand Oaks, CA: Corwin.

Harris, Alma, and Michelle Jones. 2010. "Professional Learning Communities and System Improvement." *Improving Schools* 13, no. 2: 172–81.

Hilliard, Ann Toler, and Edward Newsome Jr. 2013. "Effective Communication and Creating Professional Learning Communities Is a Valuable Practice for Superintendents." *Contemporary Issues in Education Research* 6, no. 4: 353–64.

McCarley, Troy A., Michelle L. Peters, and John M. Decman. 2016. "Transformational Leadership Related to School Climate: A Multi-level Analysis." *Educational Management Administration and Leadership* 44, no. 2 (March): 322–42.

Nelson, Tamara Holmlund, Linda LeBard, and Charlotte Waters. 2010. "How to Create a Professional Learning Community." *Science and Children* 47, no. 9 (July): 36–40.

Rafferty, Timothy J. 2003. "School Climate and Teacher Attitudes toward Upward Communication in Secondary Schools." *American Secondary Education* 31, no. 2 (Spring): 49–70.

Siano, Jaclyn. 2018. "The Principal Benefits of Professional Learning Communities." Inspired Instruction. Retrieved from https://www.inspiredinstruction.com/post/the-principal-benefits-of-professional-learning-communities.

Stoll, Louise, Ray Bolam, Agnes McMahon, Mike Wallace, and Sally M. Thomas. 2006. "Professional Learning Communities: A Review of the Literature." *Journal of Educational Change* 7, no. 4 (January): 221–58.

Chapter 12

SEL Implications for School Leaders

COMMUNAL VALUES

Leaders must be able to speak about their core values as they seek to make an enduring, positive impact on their communities. Individuals' core values—the deep-seeded core principles that guide them—ultimately drive their decision-making process. Leaders make decisions that impact their teams, their communities, and students. Often, they are confronted with seemingly impossible, troublesome decisions that must be made, because if they are not, life will continue to unfold and determine an outcome for them.

In those moments, leaders' emotions can impact their decision-making processes. It is essential, then, that leaders at all levels within public school systems are equipped with the necessary skills to interact both socially and emotionally. As such, SEL is the crucial skill all individuals, including leaders, need to cultivate.

When leaders focus on improving their SEL competencies, they send a clear message to their team: Emotional health is just as valid as any other measure of health and well-being. To make a productive contribution to the workplace, all staff must have their social and emotional needs addressed in their school settings.

Schools are, after all, communal organizations. When members of a community can regulate their emotional status, their communities become more poised and functional. They foster empathy and grace for the human conditions of sociality and emotionality. To that end, school leaders need to incorporate SEL into their strategies to engage teaching staff and elevate SEL competencies to the same level as academic and school performance.

Chapter 12

THE VITAL WORK

SEL belongs to the category of *the* vital work all school leaders need to embrace as one of their key initiatives—first within the district's key leadership team, then among school-based leadership, and lastly among site-specific teams (schools, departments, school-specific teams, etc.). Leadership has long accepted the importance of certain tasks as vital to the success of the school. Leadership's vision, plan, and initiatives to cultivate a productive learning environment are all critical to a thriving school.

The creation of a supportive and emotionally intelligent school community should be elevated to this level. It must be grounded in genuine actions with a full-throated embrace of SEL and a clear understanding, instead of mere lip service, that undergirds the educational leaders' ability to improve the emotional health of their schools.

Social isolation, a worrying trend that was accelerated to crisis level during the COVID-19 pandemic, has induced what can be thought of as a social-emotional ability gap that spans society. Isolation and the erosion of emotional health are threatening to degrade both the quality of education and the communal value that schools produce. The signs of trouble are everywhere, from declining test scores, learning gaps, and increased absenteeism to teacher shortages, rising violence, and the politicization of education.

The implication for school leadership is therefore clear: There are broader social, economic, and political pressures straining the education system. SEL offers a powerful tool to improve the dire state of schools that must serve as academic hubs of knowledge-based learning while simultaneously attending to the communal call to nurture students as whole human beings.

Even though school system structures vary greatly, they commonly include a central office, a group of building leaders/principals, and school-based leadership teams. When SEL is applied with fidelity for an enduring impact, all levels of school leadership are required to incorporate the SEL competencies—self-awareness, self-management, responsible decision-making, relationship skills, and social awareness—into their leadership practices. This ensures meaningful, enduring changes for students, staff, and schools.

SEL IMPLICATIONS FOR DISTRICT LEADERS

District leadership starts with the superintendent's office and may include various district-level departments such as human resources, teaching for learning, technology, communications, and equity and outreach. Regardless of a department's function, SEL is foundational for all levels of leadership within a school district's central office.

As this is the central team for an entire school system, any SEL initiative must begin at this level. District leaders are critical in developing strategies and SEL initiatives that are actionable with building-level leaders—assistant principals, principals, instructional coaches—who then lead their school teams through the journey of SEL implementation.

A district's superintendent must first identify SEL as a key initiative. Many state laws already insist upon this. After SEL is determined as a key initiative, a district-level leadership team can begin to create a plan for SEL within their district. Such a plan should include the state of SEL in the district's schools as they are currently able to describe with available data (including data relevant to attendance, student/family surveys, student behavior, and participation in school activities/events). If no data can be clearly identified, a plan to generate baseline data, perhaps through a student SEL survey, would be prudent to put in place.

District leaders should then analyze the available data with the goal of identifying potential problem statements (such as, "Nearly half of seniors did not feel supported by at least one adult at school"). From there, district teams can align specific solution-oriented action steps to address the identified problems. District-level resources such as curricula that specifically address SEL student needs and competencies can then be realigned, identified, or researched for implementation.

Moreover, district-level leaders are simultaneously charged with analyzing SEL data metrics for both staff and students. Staff surveys, attendance/absence trends, and participation in school initiatives, committees, and events should be evaluated so that district leaders can "walk the talk." District (or state) leaders cannot insist on SEL as a vital focal point within our school buildings while denying that very same focus for their adult staff members. SEL is a whole human need, and a school can only truly thrive when the needs of both staff and students are taken seriously.

SEL IMPLICATIONS FOR BUILDING LEADERS

At the building level, leaders—specifically the principal and assistant principal—will be tasked to follow their district-level leaders into the SEL implementation journey. They will need to become partners as they model and infuse SEL into their own interactions as leaders at different levels within the system. Creating common team expectations is foundational for SEL; district and school leaders are not excused from doing this. Before embarking on SEL work, a consensus on team norms is essential. District-level leadership teams often bring their norms to their work with building-level leaders. Feedback from building leaders should also be sought out and incorporated into the SEL initiative.

A key shift is to embed SEL principles within the team of district- and building-level leaders. Norms among leadership teams may need to be drastically updated to truly reflect that SEL engenders safe and nurturing learning environments. At the very least, SEL should require leaders to pause and reflect on their existing systems and structures for collegial leadership collaboration: Do the structures in place ensure that all leaders feel seen, heard, and valued? Are there any current practices that may harm or indirectly silence historically underrepresented leaders, including leaders of color, female leaders, or leaders from the LGBTQIA+ community?

After building-level leaders have partnered with district-level leaders to ensure their shared understanding of SEL, they can share the work with their school team. Just as the district leaders must first partner with the building leaders, building leaders will want to consider establishing an SEL-focused school leadership team that drives the SEL work on their campuses. This may or may not be an existing school-based leadership or behavioral team. If a new team is conceived solely for SEL, it will be incumbent upon the school principal to lead the implementation of SEL into all aspects of the school culture. When a school's staff feels supported, the students feel it as well.

There is ample opportunity for SEL to be intentionally implemented and modeled on school campuses, as there are so many emotionally burdened children who need adult support. Building leaders are constantly being observed and frequently pulled into conversations with students and staff; therefore, principals must be equipped with the emotional intelligence required to navigate difficult situations at a moment's notice. Likewise, district leaders must be prepared to build the principals' capacity for SEL so the school teams can successfully address their SEL needs.

SEL IMPLICATIONS FOR SCHOOL TEAMS

Under the guidance of their principal, a school-based team is essential to implement school-specific and culturally responsive SEL practices. SEL is an avenue for students and staff to see themselves represented in the school environment. A school is more than a combination of students and teachers. Similarly, the process of education is not merely the production of academic knowledge and learning. A school is both its own community and an extension of the broader community within which it is located.

The important role a school plays in imparting norms, values, and social-emotional competencies cannot be understated. A well-conceived and well-executed SEL initiative prioritizes the responsibilities of this role and actively seeks to incorporate the unique needs of their community.

A truly impactful SEL program provides school staff and students with more tools to foster a supportive and emotionally healthy environment that nurtures the flourishing of its students. If the program is perceived as yet another burdensome requirement placed upon the staff, it cannot prove to have the intended impact or provide the skills both students and staff need.

Chapter 13

SEL Competencies for Educators and Students

SEL hits the crux of our human condition: When we assemble in social groups, we naturally have social-emotional needs and we will address them in real time, regardless of whether we have a common language to explore them. However, there is a clear need to develop a culture with a common language so that all staff and students understand the importance of SEL and address their social-emotional needs more effectively.

Student input during discussions provides perspectives into aspects such as integrating SEL skills into the current curriculum. These discussions improve student awareness of social issues that disrupt their learning and how to best address them; they are invited to be participants at the table to address issues that pertain primarily to them, which in turn validates them as contributive members of the school community.

When teachers are offered professional development and resources to incorporate SEL into their classrooms, they are better equipped to engage the students in such problem-solving and decision-making processes.

A CALL FOR LEADERSHIP

The administration sets the tone for SEL practices in a school. While it is often easy for ELA teachers to incorporate SEL in their lessons, teachers in other subjects such as math and special education can do so as well. These teachers can observe the direct impact of SEL on their students and their students' need to improve these skills. Students are more likely to stay engaged and work harder for the teachers who show they care about getting to know the students.

School leadership should pursue an initiative to advance schoolwide learner outcomes because of their desire to nurture well-informed and well-rounded

Table 13.1. Schoolwide Learner Outcomes

Critical Thinkers	Effective Communicators	Responsible Citizens	Self-Directed Learners	Technological Learners
Describe, analyze, and interpret a variety of perspectives before making judgments.	Write and speak using academic language in individual and collaborative settings.	Understand their role as a contributing member of the community, country, and world.	Manage time effectively. Choose appropriate tools to perform a task.	Effectively use digital tools and technology. Know when to use technology and for what purpose.
Synthesize information from multiple sources in pursuit of solutions.	Demonstrate active listening and critical reading skills.	Engage in a healthy lifestyle by choosing nutritious foods, staying physically fit, and caring for physical and emotional needs.	Engage in productive struggle. Create and pursue educational, vocational, and personal goals.	Self-monitor habits that sustain and improve membership in digital communities.
Reflect on one's own thinking and learning process.	Share developing ideas to promote discussion. Ask relevant questions about each other's thinking.	Demonstrate caring, tolerance, and empathy that guides behavior toward others, property, school, and community. Practice self-control and resolve conflicts through positive, non-violent actions.	Reflect upon and evaluate strengths and weaknesses.	Assess sources for credibility.

Roosevelt. (2021). Roosevelt High School Counseling. Retrieved from https://trcounseling.weebly.com/school-profile

students for the modern world. To promote this focus on improved learners, the principal can provide teachers with a schoolwide learner outcomes poster.

DAILY USE OF SEL

Teachers should display objectives in relation to SEL competencies. For instance, they can use magnets as daily lesson objectives to describe the skills they intend to use in any given lesson. Table 13.1 depicts the skills that may lead to successful schoolwide learner outcomes. These skills include critical thinking, effective communication, responsible citizenry, self-directed learning, and technological learning.

The most applicable definitions to SEL are effective communicators, responsible citizens, and self-directed learners. Students can create these definitions in a committee, and their active involvement in creating these skills will motivate students to adhere to them. Every class can focus on a different SEL skill, ranging from self-management to social awareness and relationship skills.

Table 13.1 came from one of the schools where observations took place in classrooms. The schoolwide learner outcomes were posted in every classroom and mentioned in lesson objectives. Some teachers had magnets to correlate with each outcome so that students were aware of the outcome they were learning each day. Another method is to ask students to choose which learner outcome they would like to focus on in future lessons. These activities are effective ways to engage students in simple SEL practices.

Having students develop their own mini-lessons according to a schoolwide learner outcome of their choosing is another way to engage them in important life skills. They can collaborate with others and learn from each other with a new perspective. This activity also encourages them to be more aware of how important their role is as students and how these skills relate to their daily lives. When students do not interact with the content, they are less likely to acknowledge it. Isolated content just become words on the board or on the wall and will be ignored by students.

Posters are a great way to integrate SEL into the content so that it does not appear forced. It is helpful to discuss the posters in the classroom so students know the purpose behind them. When SEL is referenced in the classroom, both in writing and in verbal instruction, students are more likely to trust its inherent value in the learning process.

School leaders seek to address many gaps in student lives that are not academic. Some student populations lead challenging lives. They may live in neighborhoods where parents are incarcerated, gangs are present, and drugs are prevalent. Some students may live in group homes, and others may be undocumented immigrants who are at risk of deportation. Students living in such conditions are less likely to be academically prepared. If the teachers do not teach SEL skills to these students, who will?

It is the responsibility of the principal and the staff to bridge the learning gap between students' knowledge and the use of SEL. There are many competing demands on teacher time that make SEL integration into the curriculum problematic and cause conflict with the administration. For example, school departments often receive new curricular standards in their disciplines from the district and it can be an uphill battle. Disciplines are at various stages in obtaining new curriculum and varying standards; now we want to throw SEL in. It is difficult to tell teachers that SEL is not something new, that it is not an addition to what they are already doing, and that they have already been incorporating it into their teaching without realizing it. Not all teachers recognize skills such as organization, goal setting, and relationships as SEL traits.

Schools with many students of low socioeconomic status have increased demands placed upon them with their at-risk student populations, which makes SEL particularly challenging. Additionally, time constraints make it even more difficult for staff to fully address SEL in the classroom.

Social workers, psychologists, social-emotional workers, and counselors are extremely strategic in bridging the gap in SEL, particularly for at-risk students. They can have the student conversations that the teachers—who often deal with thirty-five or more students in each class—do not have the time for. It is unfortunate that there are not enough staff members trained in these vital roles. Some teachers do not believe that it is within their scope of training, responsibility, or ability to address some social-emotional concerns. It is the help of these personnel that makes teaching SEL more approachable and attainable.

METHODS TO USE IN SEL

Issues arise in explaining the feasibility of SEL to hesitant teachers who are overburdened with adapting new curricula. Once the administration effectively communicates the feasibility of SEL and how it may function alongside new curricula, teachers will be more apt to include them. For SEL instruction to become mainstream, it cannot be seen as another box to check or an additional burden to the teacher's already demanding role.

Administrators need an approach to SEL that is initiated by a strong call from the administration to use SEL in the classroom. When the administrators are passionate about SEL work and knowledgeable about its usage, it can unfold more naturally in the school. SEL can be used across various subject areas and be varied according to the teachers and their teaching philosophies.

Schools can provide opportunities for teachers and administrators to discuss SEL assessment data in a cohesive and approachable manner. Culture and climate teams or similar entities can address the SEL skills the school considers as most important—possible disciplinary actions—and involve multiple school staff, including security in the narrative. Various interventions such as self-management, self-awareness, and self-efficacy can be prescribed for each SEL skill. Self-management is the most practical skill to approach.

An intervention and a solution can be created by a disciplinary matrix committee and collaborate on consistent disciplinary actions at the time of data collection. The campus security can likewise play a vital role in shaping the school's culture and climate by providing feedback on the students. A security staff's ability to participate in a disciplinary matrix committee or a similar team can motivate them to do their job to the best of their ability because they feel they have a voice and more of an impact on student learning.

Security staff can use SEL terms, which encourages them to address student misbehavior in a positive language instead of reacting in a hostile manner. Breathing and "naming to taming" (labeling emotions to regulate them) are effective methods teachers and administrators can use to guide students to reduce stress.

The 4-7-8 breathing technique is especially useful during a stressful time or before a test: Breathe in for four counts, hold it for seven, and then breathe out for eight. In this exercise, students are forced to focus on the numbers instead of what is upsetting them. This exercise can be beneficial for both students and teachers who have difficulty controlling their emotions.

This level of support also provides teachers the opportunity to socially and emotionally develop as educators. When teachers have the time and space to develop their own SEL skills, they are more likely to become models for students who need stable authority figures in their lives.

A variety of approaches can be used by teachers to enhance the SEL knowledge of the students. These approaches can be demonstrated through labs, presentations, group collaborative work, and class discussions. Throughout all these activities, teachers may hold student-led discussions that encourage the students to think for themselves.

Teachers should be flexible and change their approach from year to year to best meet their students' needs. They should use polite language and teamwork as motivators for students to perform well. Regardless of differences in subject area and types of lesson objectives, SEL approaches stay the same because they create student-focused lessons.

Administrators and teachers need conflict-resolution training through programs such as those offered by the Arbinger Institute. School leaders need their own instincts and experiences, not just mentors. They need real tools that can be relied upon when addressing conflicts at school.

The Arbinger Institute conducts trainings for police officers and teachers to better deal with deescalating conflicts. The Arbinger Pyramid of Influence presents a framework for the process of changing the ways in which we handle conflicts. When a conversation or situation is headed in a bad direction, we can think of where we need to go on the pyramid to improve the situation (Arbinger Institute 2015).

The first step of the Arbinger Pyramid of Influence is "getting outside of the box," or avoiding one's own narrow way of thinking and putting oneself in the other person's situation. In a classroom conflict, this means looking at the situation from the student's perspective. This step helps the teacher better understand *why* the student is reacting in this way—which directly correlates with empathy. The next step is to build a relationship with the student to create a positive environment. Then, to avoid conflict, the teacher should listen to the student's concerns and learn from his or her perspective.

Once these steps are completed, the educator can teach and communicate his or her own concerns to the student. The last step is to reteach or correct the student. This should only be done after the other steps are completed to avoid unnecessarily escalating a situation.

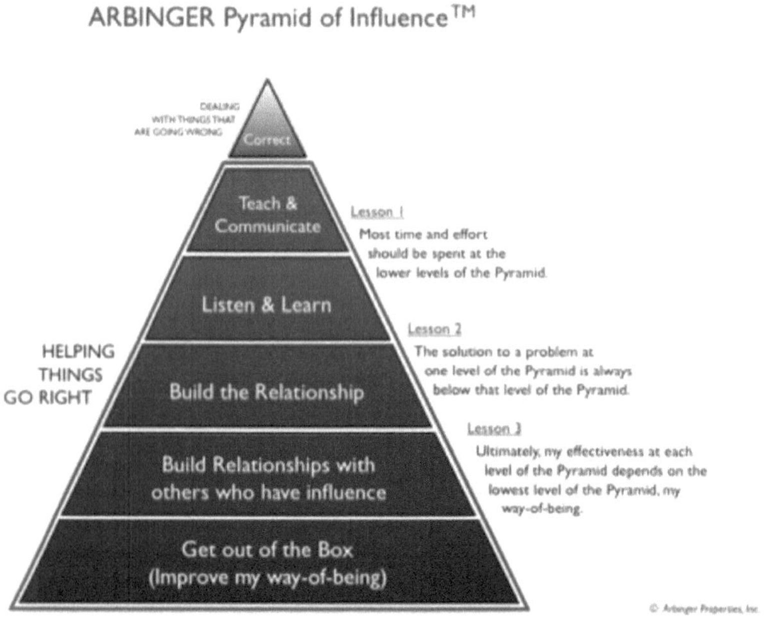

ARBINGER Pyramid of Influence™

DEALING WITH THINGS THAT ARE GOING WRONG
- Correct
- Teach & Communicate
- Listen & Learn
- Build the Relationship
- Build Relationships with others who have influence
- Get out of the Box (Improve my way-of-being)

HELPING THINGS GO RIGHT

Lesson 1
Most time and effort should be spent at the lower levels of the Pyramid.

Lesson 2
The solution to a problem at one level of the Pyramid is always below that level of the Pyramid.

Lesson 3
Ultimately, my effectiveness at each level of the Pyramid depends on the lowest level of the Pyramid, my way-of-being.

© Arbinger Properties, Inc.

Figure 13.1. ARBINGER Pyramid of Influence. Source: Arbinger Institute. (2015). *The anatomy of peace: Resolving the heart of conflict.* Oakland, CA: Berrett-Koehler Publishers, Inc." The citation from Roosevelt High School is for the table on page 124.

When building a relationship and making connections with others are not possible, simply listening and observing helps. When students can no longer approach someone with relationship building and listening skills, teachers can model behavior and effectively communicate how to handle conflict. When clear communication no longer works, teachers must correct, reteach, and practice behaviors.

In general, there are not enough staff to support the social-emotional needs of a large population of students. Many schools do not have enough psychologists, social workers, and counselors. The ones who are available have long waiting lists to meet with students. They must triage their caseloads, in many cases delaying critical responses. When there is a lack of resources and staff to support the students at school, community volunteers can serve as conflict-resolution counselors.

Tutoring through after-school programs and Khan Academy, an online platform that works in collaboration with the College Board, provides academic support for the students. The purpose of these programs is to level the playing field by giving students more targeted strategic interventions that they would not otherwise seek independently.

The SEL operation at schools involves counselors, teachers, and administrators working together to help instill the SEL skills students need for success. Magnet and STEM programs attract students. Technology is vital for students to access such programs as the Khan Academy courses that make difficult subjects more relatable to all students.

Someone walking into an SEL-focused campus or classroom can immediately sense the palpable connection among individuals. There is a difference in the conversation, engagement, and attention of the students in relation to the instruction and to one another during group interactions. There is a different level of respect and understanding.

The operation of SEL varies because certain educators interact with their students more than others. The relational capacity of the teacher is decisive in creating ease of subject-area teaching. Real-world examples create a tangible understanding of the topics, although this is not required. Nonetheless, the overarching goal of incorporating SEL into the classroom is to develop whole citizens who can relate to one another while being motivated, persistent, and empathetic.

Some educators consider themselves content area experts and do not feel comfortable incorporating SEL into their lesson plans, especially because they did not learn about it in their teacher preparation programs. Unfortunately, many secondary teachers across the country do not receive SEL preparation because it is viewed as something that should be attained in elementary school. Elementary school teachers typically receive SEL preparation because it is an essential part of their curriculum for teaching schoolwide cultural expectations.

There is a need for SEL in all subjects, including difficult-to-teach subjects such as math. Math teachers can use their content to deliver more connections through real-world examples and personal experiences. The hurdle arises with educators who are concerned that they themselves do not have the prerequisite skills to address socioemotional problems in students' lives. Educators who share this concern must understand that they have likely already included SEL in their classroom at some level; therefore, they should be trained to understand SEL to leverage what they are already doing in their classrooms.

Many humanities (generally, ELA, social studies, and the arts) teachers are interested in integrating SEL in their curriculum because they can see the direct impact it has on their students, who are already revealing themselves in their writing and other expressive work. SEL allows humanities students to feel that their voices are being heard, and they are more likely to connect with the teacher and the subject. This connection intrinsically motivates them to learn more and perform well—if not for themselves, then for their caring educator.

In addition to addressing SEL in specific content area staff meetings, separate trainings for science and math teachers can be extremely beneficial. SEL lesson plans that are sent out schoolwide approximately a week before they are implementive would be the most effective, because this gives teachers enough time to review them. It is acceptable to combine social studies, humanities, world languages, art, and similar content area expert teachers into a category of SEL trainings and then provide separate SEL training for computer science, science, and math-related disciplines.

Administrators should observe classrooms for the sole purpose of examining the SEL use in individual classroom settings; this provides them with a more thorough understanding of its current use by content area. Educators and administrators can identify and support students' needs through such activities as annotating mindset-related articles, researching potential occupations, and simulating a world war. All these activities provide opportunities for important discussions fueled by exigency.

The Right Approach

SEL must be purposeful within the community, school administration, and staff. All these parties must prioritize SEL equally for it to have the most positive effects. Student voice is particularly vital for the continued improvement of SEL at the high school level, especially in fostering students' connection to the school. Professional development is important for difficult subject areas such as math. Culture, purpose, priorities, and goals of the administration are the largest contributors to long-term SEL success at the school.

American teenagers are suffering from depression, anxiety, and suicide now more than ever. Children from upper-middle-class families and higher are overprotected, overscheduled, and overparented. Children of lower socio-economic status have more adverse childhood experiences.

The adage "Prepare the child for the road, not the road for the child" is particularly relevant for today's society because we have collectively been preparing the road for children instead of preparing children for the road (Haidt and Lukianoff 2019). Children are prone to emotional reasoning, and they need cognitive and social skills to regulate their emotional reasoning to face life's challenges. The internet especially guarantees that children deal with misinformation all the way to adulthood and beyond, but unlike many adults, they do not have the knowledge to fact-check.

Children need cognitive behavioral therapy or techniques (Haidt and Lukianoff 2019). Educators and parents can encourage children to hear their negative thoughts in a comical voice, which will make them create less clout. This technique can help both children and adults. When practicing cognitive behavioral therapy techniques, it is important to ask questions regarding negative thoughts, such as: What are the facts? Can you change your perspective?

Educators can encourage students to learn mindfulness techniques, or the practice of paying attention in the present moment without judgment (Haidt and Lukianoff 2019). Mindful practices reduce anxiety and stress while enhancing coping, compassion, and emotional regulation.

There are many ways schools and educators can create a return to learning in a free space. One such suggestion is to provide less homework in early grades and encourage more play and creativity. Longer assignments do not serve this age well. More recess with less adult supervision and after-school play clubs allow students to have more free time.

A no-device policy where devices are placed in cubbies or lockers can encourage students to focus on learning and free play. Many middle schools have done away with recess to focus more on academics. A return to offering recess in middle school where possible could facilitate exercise, peer relationships, and creativity (Haidt and Lukianoff 2019).

Educators can use more debates in class or sponsor debate clubs to encourage an intellectual framework for students to practice presenting and supporting arguments. Educators can also assign readings and coursework that promote reasoned discussion to encourage advanced thinking. Class discussions around this type of thinking will encourage students to develop their rational thoughts.

Suggestions for a Gap Year

Students should be encouraged to take a gap year after high school, especially those who are uncertain about what to study in college or whether to attend college at all. Students who are not ready for a gap year after high school could consider taking one after earning a degree to ensure that they are embarking on the correct career path. Whenever it is taken, a gap year fosters personal growth and career exploration.

During a gap year, students can do a year of service. Part-time work or a full-time job can help prepare students for college. They should be motivated by both parents and educators to take such opportunities to develop as whole people.

Community Focus and Systemic Realignment

There also needs to be a return to community. Students today are more isolated than previous generations, which stunts their social interactions and developmental growth (Haidt and Lukianoff 2019). Community allows students to bounce ideas and learn from elders who have served in the roles that they are considering.

When the modern education system was designed in the nineteenth and twentieth centuries, its creators believed that there was a need to develop talent and skills. Today, COVID-19, recession, racialized violence, and inequities in opportunity among our youth have adversely impacted the education system. However, there is a silver lining: We can create an education system that serves all children (Cantor 2021). SEL can be a permanent solution to these ills instead of just a temporary quick-fix.

Learning happens everywhere, all the time, in all types of settings. Neither public schools nor youth development organizations can fully address the whole child or involve the whole community. Talents and skills are equal, and education should be designed to reveal the talents and skills of every child (Cantor 2021).

We can design a system that instills talent and potential, one where all young people can thrive. There needs to be a transformational shift to fulfill the ultimate purpose and potential of our learning systems. In the light of recent global events, we can discontinue the systems and laws that constrain this transformational vision that is grounded in what we know about human development, the development of the brain, and learning choices (Cantor 2021).

Human connection matters, and global challenges have made teaching SEL more essential than ever before. Educators have a unique opportunity to make a difference in the lives of all students, who need at least one caring adult in their lives.

The importance of SEL unquestionably rests with the ability to advance learner outcomes. While it may be easier to reach students socially and emotionally in particular subject areas (such as the humanities), there is a need for all staff members to be trained to teach SEL. This training will educate teachers to implement the Arbinger Pyramid of Influence's main purpose, which is to build relationships and listen before correcting behavior through instruction in their content area classes.

Students must interact with SEL content for true buy-in to occur, and SEL should be reinforced in writing as well as in person. Lesson objectives that relate to SEL—either with magnets or written on the board—can drive the interest and focus of the students. Students can be invited to create SEL or citizen-like terms in a classroom committee. The traits that they create together can be referenced all year long to promote a culture that they participated in building.

Relieving Teachers

SEL can reduce the burden faced by teachers by reducing the time they spend dealing with misbehavior and discipline issues, which allows more time to focus on content. There needs to be a strong calling from the administration to use SEL in the classroom for the sake of students and teachers. Techniques such as 4-7-8 breathing provide simple ways to integrate SEL with content. Educators should regularly adjust their lessons to meet student needs, and SEL can assist with that adjustment process.

There is not enough support staff to meet the SEL needs of all students. Targeting strategic innovations to make up for this lack of support allows for student voices to be heard. Children must be prepared for whatever the future may hold. Unfortunately, misinformation is prolific. Therefore, students must be taught how to discern between fact and fiction, particularly online. SEL is a permanent rather than temporary solution to societal issues, and we need to start treating SEL as the permanent solution that it is.

Controversial Issues in Education

The fixation on testing and its dire effects on learning have continued in recent years, even through the COVID-19 pandemic. Teachers who were considered heroes in 2020 were vilified in 2022. Extremists are exploiting anxiety and uncertainty to undermine education. One example of this is tip lines where parents and students can report teachers for teaching what they considered to be critical race theory, transgenderism, or any other controversial topic

(Boone, Erinakes, and Ferroni 2022). The LGBTQIA+ student community has also been targeted. In essence, students of all identities are not authentically welcomed in every school space—which is antithetical to SEL.

Students should develop empathy instead of shame when they learn about slavery. Many critics believe that schools may create a wave of shame among white students by discussing slavery and its effects on contemporary race relations. In fact, it is quite the opposite: Students should feel empathetic toward the ancestors of their African American peers.

Education is an equalizer that provides a voice, agency, and empowerment to all learners (Boone Erinakes, and Ferroni 2022). Educators have been rising to the occasion while rebuilding relationships with students, even as they struggle to keep up with the same curriculum pacing guides and assessments they were burdened with prior to the pandemic.

In 2022, between one-half and two-thirds of teachers considered leaving the profession (Boone Erinakes, and Ferroni 2022), and the reasons are many. The workload has increased exponentially and teacher morale is at an all-time low. Many schools have faced COVID outbreaks, and many staff are immunocompromised, leading to high levels of anxiety.

There is a severe teacher shortage because teachers do not feel safe or supported, and they are overwhelmed. Many teachers feel they have faced repercussions in terms of their livelihood, sanity, and family life due to all these taxing events (Boone Erinakes, and Ferroni 2022).

Some educators are working sixty to seventy hours a week without an increase in salary or benefits. In fact, some localities have decreased pay, removed years of service, or frozen pay—all at a time when educators needed an increase the most. There is a widening of racial and economic divides, which often correlates with a "haves and have-nots" mindset that continues to permeate our society. Many teachers work multiple part-time jobs to be able to support their families.

Throughout the first two years of the pandemic, students remained at home. Teachers had to simultaneously teach online and in-person—and were expected do both effectively. This caused some "double planning," as needs cannot be met in the same manner in the classroom and virtually. There has been a shortage of substitutes, leaving many teachers to cover their colleagues' classes or combine classes in their absence, resulting in larger class sizes. This causes more stress because of the increased number of student behavioral issues.

The 2021–2022 school year was overwhelming, mentally draining, and exhausting for many educators (Boone Erinakes, and Ferroni 2022). Many expected it would be easier after a year of virtual learning; conversely, it was worse because of the "learning loss" combined with a social-emotional learning delay.

The learning loss was quite significant because of the lack of in-person instruction and the ability to physically be around peers. Students forgot how to be students. They forgot how to interact with one another. Even some adults have forgotten how to interact with their peers.

Closing Thoughts

During the pandemic, some schools could not provide computers for all their students, and many students had no internet access at home. Family members of many students and educators lost their jobs. Many also faced the loss of family members to COVID. When students and teachers returned to in-person learning, educators' anxiety was extremely high because there were many unanswered questions (Boone Erinakes, and Ferroni 2022).

Students need healthy teachers. They also need social workers and school psychologists. There are not enough of these professionals. Every single day, teachers invest in their students, financially, emotionally, and socially. Teachers want society to invest as much in them and in their schools as they do in their students. If teachers cannot attain social-emotional balance in their own lives, it may indeed be time to find a new profession.

The two philosophies of Hobbes and Rousseau describe the two most influential perspectives within education. Hobbes theorized that developing the child for society was the best course of action. It gave the future adult purpose and a role to fit into. Meanwhile, Rousseau believed children have natural wisdom and should not be molded to fit into society. Rather they should be allowed to just "be," so that they can find themselves first. Hobbes is the equivalent of the modern college- and career-oriented education philosopher, while Rousseau is the equivalent of the modern heart and ready education philosopher.

Strong leadership and a collaborative culture set by the district and administrative leaders are essential for the long-term success of the school. Overall, most educators and education leaders view SEL as beneficial to their students' education, even if it means increased workloads for themselves. Educators provide an irreplaceable service by striving to develop their students socially and emotionally.

Character is arguably more important than personality when considering the effects of an individual on society. Character is what drives decision-making that immediately affects others. According to the Myers-Briggs Type Indicator, Adolf Hitler and Martin Luther King Jr. had the same personality; the difference was in their character.

Society is better served when actions are grounded in character. When peoples' strengths are grounded in emotional and intellectual competencies, we all benefit. We need people to make right, just, and moral decisions that benefit society. When we raise kids to make responsible decisions with a strong character, we are helping not just them, but everyone—even those yet to be born. Kids *are* the content and content is nothing without character.

REFERENCES

Arbinger Institute. 2015. *The Anatomy of Peace: Resolving the Heart of Conflict.* Oakland, CA: Berrett-Koehler.

Boone, Monique, Kelly Erinakes, and Nicholas Ferroni. 2022. "Revitalizing the Teaching Profession: Three Educators Share Their Experiences and Aspirations." *American Educator* 46, no. 2 (Summer). https://www.aft.org/ae/summer2022/boone_erinakes_ferroni.

Cantor, Pamela. 2021. "All Children Thriving: A New Purpose for Education." *American Educator* 45, no. 3 (Fall): 14–26.

Haidt, Jonathan, and Greg Lukianoff. 2019. *The Coddling of the American Mind: How Good Intentions and Bad Ideas Are Setting Up a Generation for Failure.* Harlow, UK: Penguin.

Roosevelt High School Counseling. n.d. "School Profile." Retrieved from https://trcounseling.weebly.com/school-profile.

References

Arbinger Institute. 2015. *The Anatomy of Peace: Resolving the Heart of Conflict.* Oakland, CA: Berrett-Koehler.
Bilmes, Jenna. 2012. *Beyond Behavior Management: The Six Life Skills Children Need.* 2nd ed. St. Paul, MN: Redleaf Press.
Biscotti, Nicole. 2021. *I Can Learn When I'm Moving: Going to School with ADHD.* Quincy, MA: EduMarch.
Boone, Monique, Kelly Erinakes, and Nicholas Ferroni. 2022. "Revitalizing the Teaching Profession: Three Educators Share Their Experiences and Aspirations." *American Educator* 46, no. 2 (Summer). https://www.aft.org/ae/summer2022/boone_erinakes_ferroni.
Borba, Michele. 2016. *UnSelfie: Why Empathetic Kids Succeed in Our All-About-Me World.* New York: Touchstone.
Bregman, Rutger. 2019. *Humankind: A Hopeful History.* New York: Little, Brown.
Brendtro, Larry, and Lesley du Toit. 2005. *Response Ability Pathways: Restoring Bonds of Respect.* Cape Town, South Africa: Pretext.
Brewer, Judson. 2021. *Unwinding Anxiety: New Science Shows How to Break the Cycles of Worry and Fear to Heal Your Mind.* New York: Avery.
Brown, Brené. 2015. *Rising Strong.* New York: Penguin Random House.
Brown, Brené. 2021. *Atlas of the Heart: Mapping Meaningful Connection and the Language of Human Experience.* New York: Random House.
Cantor, Pamela. 2021. "All Children Thriving: A New Purpose for Education." *American Educator* 45, no. 3 (Fall): 14–26.
Corliss, Julia Candace, and Aaron Dahlgren. 2018. *Unconditional Positive Regard: The Science, Psychology, and Strategies behind High-Performing Classrooms.* Hayden Lake, ID: Center for Teacher Effectiveness.
Cuban, Larry. 1998. "How Schools Change Reforms: Redefining Reform Success and Failure." *Teachers College Record* 99, no. 3 (Spring): 453–77.
Dahlgren, Rick, and Judy Hyatt. 2007. *Time to Teach: Encouragement, Empowerment, and Excellence in Every Classroom with Refocus.* Hayden Lake, ID: Center for Teacher Effectiveness.
Dick, Danielle M. 2021. *The Child Code: Understanding Your Child's Unique Nature for Happier, More Effective Parenting.* New York: Avery.

Duckworth, Angela. 2016. *Grit: The Power of Passion and Perserverance*. New York: Scribner.

Duckworth, Angela L., and Martin E. P. Seligman. 2005. "Self-discipline Outdoes IQ Predicting Academic Performance in Adolescents." *Psychological Science* 16, no. 12 (December): 939–44.

Dweck, Carol S. 2006. *Mindset: The New Psychology of Success*. New York: Random House.

Faber, Adele, and Elaine Mazlish. 1980. *How to Talk So Kids Will Listen & Listen So Kids Will Talk*. New York: Scribner.

Feldman, Joe. 2019. *Grading for Equity: What It Is, Why It Matters, and How It Can Transform Schools and Classrooms*. Thousand Oaks, CA: Corwin.

Gillihan, Scott. 2018. *Cognitive Behavioral Therapy Made Simple: 10 Strategies for Managing Anxiety, Depression, Anger, Panic, and Worry*. Emeryville, CA: Althea Press.

Goleman, Daniel. 2005. *Emotional Intelligence*. New York: Bantam.

Greenland, Susan Kaiser. 2010. *The Mindful Child: How to Help Your Kid Manage Stress and Become Happier, Kinder, and More Compassionate*. New York: Atria Paperback.

Haidt, Jonathan, and Greg Lukianoff. 2019. *The Coddling of the American Mind: How Good Intentions and Bad Ideas Are Setting Up a Generation for Failure*. Harlow, UK: Penguin.

Hallowell, . 2002. *Connections*. Paper presented at the National Adolescent Conference, Scottsdale, AZ.

Hammond, Zaretta L. 2014. *Culturally Responsive Teaching and the Brain: Promoting Authentic Engagement and Rigor among Culturally and Linguistically Diverse Students*. Thousand Oaks, CA: Corwin.

Hansen, Morten T. 2018. *Great at Work: How Top Performers Do Less, Work Better, and Achieve More*. New York: Simon and Schuster.

Harris, Alma, and Michelle Jones. 2010. "Professional Learning Communities and System Improvement." *Improving Schools* 13, no. 2: 172–81.

Harvard Business Review, compiler. 2001. *Harvard Business Review on Decision Making*. Boston: Harvard Business Review Press.

Hilliard, Ann Toler, and Edward Newsome Jr. 2013. "Effective Communication and Creating Professional Learning Communities Is a Valuable Practice for Superintendents." *Contemporary Issues in Education Research* 6, no. 4: 353–64.

Hubble, Mark A., Barry L. Duncan, and Scott D. Miller. 1999. *The Heart and Soul of Change: What Works in Therapy*. Washington, DC: American Psychological Association.

Hunter, James C. 2017. *The Culture: Creating Excellence with Those You Lead By Growing Leaders and Building Community*. Banbury, UK: JDH Publishing.

Iheoma, Eugene O. 1997. "Rousseau's Views on Teaching." *Journal of Educational Thought* 31, no. 1 (April): 69–81.

Ladson-Billings, Gloria. 1994. *The Dreamkeepers: Successful Teachers of African American Children*. San Francisco: Jossey-Bass.

Laugeson, Elizabeth A. 2013. *The Science of Making Friends: Helping Socially Challenged Teens and Young Adults.* San Francisco: Jossey-Bass.

Lemov, Doug. 2015. *Teach Like a Champion 2.0: 62 Techniques That Put Students on the Path to College.* San Francisco: Joseey-Bass.

Lipman, Frank, and Neil Parikh. 2021. *Better Sleep, Better You.* New York: Little Brown Spark.

Martinez Perez, Lorea. 2020. *Teaching with the Heart in Mind: A Complete Educator's Guide to Social Emotional Learning.* New York: Brisca Publishing.

Marzano, Robert J. 2017. *The New Art and Science of Teaching.* Bloomington, IN: Solution Tree.

Mauboussin, Michael J. 2013. *Think Twice: Harnessing the Power of Counterintuition.* Boston: Harvard Business Review Press.

McCarley, Troy A., Michelle L. Peters, and John M. Decman. 2016. "Transformational Leadership Related to School Climate: A Multi-level Analysis." *Educational Management Administration and Leadership* 44, no. 2 (March): 322–42.

Mischel, Walter. 2014. *The Marshmallow Test: Mastering Self-Control.* New York: Little, Brown.

Muijs, Daniel, and David Reynolds. 2002. "Teachers' Beliefs and Behaviors: What Really Matters?" *Journal of Classroom Interaction* 37, no. 2: 3–15.

Neff, Kristin. 2011. *Self-Compassion: The Proven Power of Being Kind to Yourself.* New York: HarperCollins.

Nelson, Tamara Holmlund, Linda LeBard, and Charlotte Waters. 2010. "How to Create a Professional Learning Community." *Science and Children* 47, no. 9 (July): 36–40.

Peterson, Lloyd Douglas, K. Richard Young, Charles L. Salzberg, Richard P. West, and Mary Hill. 2006. "Using Self-Management Procedures to Improve Classroom Social Skills in Multiple General Education Settings." *Education and Treatment of Children* 29, no. 1 (February): 1–21.

Pink, Daniel H. 2009. *Drive: The Surprising Truth about What Motivates Us.* New York: Riverhead.

Rafferty, Timothy J. 2003. "School Climate and Teacher Attitudes toward Upward Communication in Secondary Schools." *American Secondary Education* 31, no. 2 (Spring): 49–70.

Roosevelt High School Counseling. n.d. "School Profile." Retrieved from https://trcounseling.weebly.com/school-profile.

Rosenberg, Marshall B. 2015. *Nonviolent Communication: A Language of Life.* Encinitas, CA: PuddleDancer Press.

Scott, Susan. 2002. *Fierce Conversations: Achieving Success at Work and in Life, One Conversation at a Time.* New York: Viking.

Siano, Jaclyn. 2018. "The Principal Benefits of Professional Learning Communities." Inspired Instruction. Retrieved from https://www.inspiredinstruction.com/post/the-principal-benefits-of-professional-learning-communities.

Siegel, Daniel J., and Tina Payne Bryson. 2012. *The Whole-Brain Child: 12 Revolutionary Strategies to Nurture Your Child's Developing Mind.* New York: Bantam.

Stevenson, Heidi, and Nancy Lourié Markowitz. 2019. "Introduction: Social Emotional Learning and Culturally Responsive and Sustaining Teaching Practices." *Teacher Education Quarterly* 46, no. 4 (Fall): 3–9.

Stoll, Louise, Ray Bolam, Agnes McMahon, Mike Wallace, and Sally M. Thomas. 2006. "Professional Learning Communities: A Review of the Literature." *Journal of Educational Change* 7, no. 4 (January): 221–58.

University of Washington College of Education. n.d. Center for Educational Leadership. Retrieved from https://k-12leadership.org/resources/?filter=framework.

Van Susteren, Lisa, and Stacey Colino. 2020. *Emotional Inflammation: Discover Your Triggers and Reclaim Your Equilibrium during Anxious Times*. Louisville, CO: Sounds True.

Watkins, Michael. 2003. *The First 90 Days: Proven Strategies for Getting up to Speed Faster and Smarter*. Boston: Harvard Business Review Press.

Wong, Harry K., and Rosemary T. Wong. 2009. *The First Days of School: How to Be an Effective Teacher*. Mountain View, CA: Harry K. Wong Publications.

Yoder, Nicholas. 2014. *Self-Assessing Social and Emotional Instruction and Competencies: A Tool for Teachers*. Washington, DC: American Institutes for Research. Retrieved from https://files.eric.ed.gov/fulltext/ED553369.pdf.

Zee, Marjolein, and Helma M. Y. Koomen. 2016. "Teacher Self-Efficacy and Its Effects on Classroom Processes, Student Academic Adjustment, and Teacher Well-Being: A Synthesis of 40 Years of Research." *Review of Educational Research* 86, no. 4 (December): 981–1015.

Index

academic skills, 72, 81
acceptance, mindfulness relation to, 22
accountability, 1, 26, 68; in high school, 32; punishments relation to, 69; to rules, 76
ACE. *See* adverse childhood experiences
achievement, culture of, 8
ADHD. *See* attention deficit hyperactivity disorder
administrators, 32, 33, 87, 109, 123, 133; feedback to, 21, 34; home visits by, 101; observation by, 130; in PLCs, 113–14; teacher support from, 19, 20
adults, 6, 16–17, 90
adverse childhood experiences (ACE), 90, 95–96
affirmation, during hardships, 17
altruistic projects, relationships from, 53
American Psychological Association (APA), 7
anxiety, 6–7, 15; from COVID-19, 134–35; extremists exploiting, 133; mindfulness effect on, 131; social media relation to, 6
APA. *See* American Psychological Association
appreciation, for student work, 25

Arbinger Institute, 127–28, 129
Arbinger Pyramid of Influence, 127–28, *128*, 129, 133
ASD. *See* autism spectrum disorder
assessments, 67, 68, 108, 115; equity in, 65–66
assistant principals, 119
at-risk student populations, 126
attachment, 92
attention, 102; emotions relation to, 41, 47; engagement relation to, 50–51
attention deficit hyperactivity disorder (ADHD), 93–94
auditory learners, 50
autism spectrum disorder (ASD), 93
autonomy, community relation to, 9

behavior, 4, 36, 42; bullying, 29, 94, 106; climate relation to, 47; cognitive behavioral therapy for, 131; expectations for, 72; genetic disposition relation to, 85–86; minimum grading practices effect on, 65; positive, 63, 68, 86; social media relation to, 49, 106. *See also* misbehaviors
bias, rubrics relation to, 66
Black families, inequities effecting, 4
blame, in Western society, 22

blank slate (*tabula rasa*), 7
Bloom's taxonomy, 61
bomb threats, 72
boundaries, 26, 43; burnout relation to, 87; decisions relation to, 59
breaks, 35, 36, 52, 81, 86; for engagement, 50; focus relation to, 54
breathing breaks, stress relieved by, 35
Brewer, Judson, 6–7
Brown, Brené, 23
building-level leaders, 119–20
bullying behavior, 29, 94, 106
burnout, 15, 20, 25, 81, 95; boundaries relation to, 87; equilibrium relation to, 45; poverty relation to, 89; relationships relation to, 92; stress relation to, 43

Capturing Kids' Hearts, 107
career path, 132
CASEL. *See* Collaborative for Academic, Social, and Emotional Learning
character, personality compared to, 135–36
CharacterStrong, 107
cheating, 65, 68
child protective services (CPS), 96–97
children. *See specific topics*
chronotypes, for sleep, 45–46
Cinnabon, 108, 109
classrooms, 3, 18, 42, 71; decorations in, 35, 61, 95; as safe space, 89; success in, 20–21, 59
climate, 42, 47, 108, 114–15; administrators effect on, 32; culture compared to, 5–6, 10; security staff effect on, 127
Clintondale, New York, 20–21
clubs, after-school play, 131
code-switching, 106
cognitive behavioral therapy, 131
Cole, Kat, 108–9
collaboration, 25, 74–75, 76, 91, 135; in group work, 65, 95, 96; in PLCs, 113; for problem-solving, 63–64; in relationships, 86; trauma relation to, 92
Collaborative for Academic, Social, and Emotional Learning (CASEL), 5, 15
college applications, of seniors, 83
College Board, 129
coloring, as brain break, 50
communication, 21, 83–84, 95, 126; in Arbinger Pyramid of Influence, 128, 129; relationships relation to, 18–19
community, 9, 53, 96, 116, 120–21, 132; isolation relation to, 132; professional learning, 113–14
conflict resolution, 91–92, 96, 127–28
conflicts, 19, 68, 83, 106–7, 115; trauma relation to, 95
connection, 82, 90, 93, 102, 103, 132–33; home-school, 9, 110; trust in, 84
consequences, 73, 86; for misbehaviors, 33, 63
consistency, 33, 36
control, 44, 45, 52, 53; of feelings, 31; freedom balanced with, 7; self, 55, 76; of stimulus, 51
controversial topics, 133–34
COVID-19, 6, 16, 64, 133; anxiety from, 134–35; burnout relation to, 25; isolation during, 118
CPS. *See* child protective services
creativity, 16, 62, 131; freedom for, 24; motivation for, 54
crisis, support in, 84–85
CRT. *See* culturally responsive teaching
Cuban, Larry, 3
culturally responsive teaching (CRT), 9, 64, 68
culture, 8, 17–18, 47, 114–15, 133; administrators effect on, 32; climate compared to, 5–6, 10; of collaboration, 135; conflicts in, 106–7; in CRT, 64; leaders relation to, 3; learning relation to, 90; rapport relation to, 9; security staff effect on, 127; surveys for, 108

curiosity, 16
current events, discussions of, 72
curriculum, 37, 119, 123; health-focused, 35
cyberbullying, 106
cybersickness, 61

decisions, 2, 10, 30, 67, 74; boundaries relation to, 59; emotions relation to, 15, 41, 60, 117; future affected by, 75; about grades, 82; isolation effect on, 43; questions effect on, 77; real-world examples relation to, 76; sleep-deprivation effect on, 53
decorations, in classrooms, 35, 61, 95
definitions, for SEL skills, 125
depression, 53, 101; play compared to, 8–9
dichotomy, in human nature, 10
did not finish (DNF), 108
diet, 46, 47
disciplinary action, 36, 92–93, 127
discussions, 72; collaboration in, 74–75; decisions affected by, 77
distractions, 44, 61
district leaders, 118–20
DNF. *See* did not finish
Duckworth, Angela L., 101, 108

early childhood, trauma in, 105
Education Week (media outlet), 3
ELA. *See* English language arts
elementary schools, 3, 36, 129
emotional intelligence, 2, 9, 15, 74, 94, 120; environment relation to, 4
Emotional Intelligence (Goleman), 15
emotional regulation, in adults, 6
emotional wake, 24, 25
emotions, 4, 18, 36, 43, 101; attention relation to, 41, 47; decisions relation to, 15, 41, 60, 117; emotional wake affected by, 25; honesty of, 84; learning relation to, 16, 18; mood meter for, 52, 55; needs relation to, 23; self-monitoring of, 54–55;
self-regulation of, 31–32, 51; of students, 86–87, 96, 105
empathy, 34, 66, 87, 128, 134; collaboration relation to, 96; judgment relation to, 83–84; listening relation to, 52; modeling of, 54–55; self-awareness relation to, 22–23; socioeconomic status relation to, 106; vulnerability relation to, 62
empathy gap, 6, 15, 25
engagement, 42, 72; connection relation to, 103; misbehaviors relation to, 50–51
English language arts (ELA), 34, 35, 83, 94, 123
enthusiasm, 42, 103
environment, 3, 4, 59, 86; in Arbinger Pyramid of Influence, 128; relationship skills affected by, 18; sharing effect on, 82, 87–88
equilibrium, 43, 45
equity, 65–66, 68
exercise, 46, 48
expectations, 22, 42, 49, 54, 109; for behavior, 72; communication of, 83
expression, of feelings, 19, 23
extra credit, 65, 68
extremists, anxiety exploited by, 133

Faber, Adele, 62–63
Father Knows Best (TV show), 75
favoritism, engagement relation to, 42
fear, 7, 10
feasibility, of SEL, 126
feedback, 50, 68, 69, 85; to administrators, 21, 34; for social awareness, 104
feelings, 60, 62; control of, 31; expression of, 19, 23; thoughts compared to, 20
fiction, empathy from, 34
firmness, 87, 88
"5 Dimensions of Teaching and Learning," University of Washington, 3

fixed mindset, growth mindset compared to, 4
focus, 46, 54, 62; prioritization relation to, 43, 47
4-7-8 breathing technique, 127, 133
fractionalizing, of intervention, 60
freedom, 7, 9, 24
friendship skills, 91, 93
future, 7, 75

gap year, 132
genetic disposition, behavior relation to, 85–86
goals, 53–54, 55, 62
Goleman, Daniel, 15, 95
grades, decisions about, 82
gratification, delay of, 52, 55
Greenland, Susan Kaiser, 29
greetings, 5, 107
grit, 109
Grit (Duckworth), 108
group work, 65, 90, 95, 96
growth mindset, 33, 65; fixed mindset compared to, 4
guest speakers, 107

Hamlet (play), 34
hardships, affirmation during, 17
health, 16, 47–48, 117
health-focused curriculum, in ELA, 35
high school, 3, 4, 9, 32
Hitler, Adolf, 135
Hobbes, Thomas, 29, 41, 52, 66, 109, 135; Rousseau compared to, 7–8, 10
home-school connections, 9, 110
home visits, by administrators, 101
homework, 65, 68, 131
honesty, of emotions, 84
Hooters, 108–9
humanities, 83, 95; student voices in, 130
human nature, 7–8, 10
hummingbird, as chronotype, 46
humor, 72, 73, 76, 131
Hunter, Madeline, 1, 5–6

icebreakers, for learning, 72
impulse-control, sleep relation to, 53
inclusion, performance outcomes relation to, 18
individualism, 8
Industrial Revolution, 8, 64
inequities, 3, 4
inner worlds, success relation to, 16–17
instruction, whole-class-directed, 49
interaction skills, in group work, 90
intervention, 59, 60, 115, 127
isolation, 43, 118, 132

journal writing, 82, 86–87
judgment, 21, 43; empathy relation to, 83–84; mindfulness relation to, 131

Khan Academy, 129
The Killing (TV show), 75
kindness, 66–67, 93, 110
kinesthetic learners, 50
King, Martin Luther, Jr., 135

language, for social-emotional needs, 123
larks, as chronotype, 45, 46
leaders, 3, 16, 123, 125–26; of districts, 118–20; success relation to, 118, 135
learning, 8, 10, 21, 72, 132; culture relation to, 90; emotions relation to, 16, 18; real-world examples for, 73; stress effect on, 89; in student-to-student interactions, 75–76; understanding relation to, 94
learning gaps, in student lives, 125–26
lectures, whole-class-directed instruction compared to, 49
lessons, 41, 102
LGBTQIA+ community, 134
Lipman, Frank, 45, 46
listening, 52, 61–62
Lord of the Flies (book), 7

magnet programs, 129
marshmallow test, 51, 52, 55

Maslow's hierarchy of needs, 61
math, 95, 130; professional development in, 131; real-world examples for, 73
Mazlish, Elaine, 62–63
meditation, 29; for mindfulness, 26, 35
mental health, remote learning relation to, 16
mindfulness, 42, 131; acceptance relation to, 22; curriculum of, 37; meditation for, 26, 35; wheel of awareness for, 29–30, 36
mindset, 17, 34, 103; growth, 4, 33, 65
minimum grading practices, 64–65, 68
misbehaviors, 31, 32, 101, 133; consequences for, 33, 63; engagement relation to, 50–51; focus affected by, 62; punishments for, 68; teacher reaction to, 74, 75; in transition grades, 19
misinformation, 131, 133
mistakes, 21, 60; self-compassion for, 22
modeling, 63, 107, 110; of empathy, 54–55; of self-control, 76
mood meter, for emotions, 52, 55
morale, of teachers, 134
morning circles, in elementary schools, 36
motivation, 42, 51, 54, 67, 85; for goals, 55; for growth mindset, 65; humor for, 73; mistakes relation to, 60; praise relation to, 63
motivational speech, 24
Multi-Tiered Systems of Support (MTSS), 5, 9
Myers-Briggs Type Indicator, 135

National Sleep Foundation, 52
needs, 23, 61
Neff, Kristin, 22
negative thought patterns, 16, 131
negativity, technology relation to, 72
networks, for support, 45
New York, Clintondale, 20–21
New Zealand, 64

ninth graders, 31, 32, 36
No Child Left Behind, 67
no-device policy, 131
nontraditional family structures, self-efficacy in, 54
nonviolent communication, 83–84
Nonviolent Communication (Rosenberg), 23–24

observation, 130; journal for, 68
organization, for self-management, 41, 47
owl, as chronotype, 46
oxytocin, 92

pandemic. *See* COVID-19
parents, 67
Parikh, Neil, 45, 46
Payne Bryson, Tina, 29–30
PBIS. *See* Positive Behavior Interventions and Supports
pedagogy, students affected by, 5
PEERS. *See* Program for the Education and Enrichment of Relational Skills
perception, of truth, 8
performance outcomes, 18, 49
personality, character compared to, 135–36
pessimistic views, depression relation to, 101
physical education, 7
"picture of the day," 82
Pink, Dan, 21, 53–54
plans, for control, 44
play, 8–9, 10
PLC. *See* professional learning community
politics, 7, 102
positive behavior, 63, 68, 86
Positive Behavior Interventions and Supports (PBIS), 5, 9, 32, 86
posters, for SEL, 29, 34, 61, 106, 125
poverty, burnout relation to, 89
praise, motivation relation to, 63
preparation, for lessons, 41

pressure, productivity affected by, 47
principals, 119–20, 123, 125; learning gaps bridged by, 126
prioritization, focus relation to, 43, 47
problem-solving, collaboration for, 63–64
procrastination, decisions relation to, 60
productivity, stress effect on, 47
professional development, 4–5, 6, 67, 116, 123; enthusiasm relation to, 103; in math, 131
professional learning community (PLC), 113–14
Program for the Education and Enrichment of Relational Skills (PEERS), 93
punishments, 63, 68, 69, 91

questions, 77, 103; for engagement, 72

Race to the Top initiative, 20
rapport, 9, 96; in classrooms, 3
reading ability, 32
reading/writing learners, 50
real-world examples, 73, 76
recess, creativity relation to, 131
reflections, 29, 82, 87, 101; for student voices, 36. *See also* self-reflection
regrets, self-compassion to eliminate, 25
relationships, 53, 81, 83, 92, 108; in Arbinger Pyramid of Influence, 128, 129; collaboration in, 86; communication relation to, 18–19; self-management relation to, 55; strategies to build, 115; trust in, 61, 85
relationship skills, 2, 5, 18
relaxation techniques, focus affected by, 46
remote learning, 16, 61, 134–35
respect, 64, 81, 84, 87
responsibility, for emotional wake, 24
restitution practices, for cheating, 65
restorative classrooms, 18
restorative justice, 115

retakes, of assessments, 66, 68
review, after breaks, 81
rigidity, 43, 47
Rising Strong (Brown), 23
risk, environment relation to, 3
risk factors, self-management of, 51
role-plays, 62, 108
Rosenberg, Marshall B., 22–23
Rousseau, Jean-Jacques, 47, 50, 66, 135; Hobbes compared to, 7–8, 10
rubrics, 66, 68
rules, 42, 71, 76

safe space, classrooms as, 89
safety, in disciplinary action, 92–93
salaries, of teachers, 67
satisfaction, self-esteem relation to, 71
school shootings, 72
Schoolwide Learner Outcomes, *124*
security staff, 34, 127
segregation, SEL effect on, 9
SEL. *See* social-emotional learning
self-actualization, goals relation to, 53–54
self-awareness, 2, 17, 29–30, 31, 34, 36; empathy relation to, 22–23; self-efficacy relation to, 49
self-compassion, 3, 21, 22, 25, 26
self-control, 55, 76
self-critic, self-reflections relation to, 22
self-efficacy, 42, 45, 47, 54; self-awareness relation to, 49; for success, 73
self-esteem, satisfaction relation to, 71
self-hatred, judgment relation to, 21
self-image, in student stories, 53
self-kindness, 22
self-management, 2, 41, 47, 49, 127; relationships relation to, 55; of risk factors, 51; success relation to, 42
self-monitoring, of emotions, 54–55
self-reflection, 22, 25, 44–45
self-regulation, 25, 31–32, 51, 52
self-talk, accountability for, 26
Seligman, Martin E. P., 101

seniors, college applications of, 83
shame, 134
sharing, environment affected by, 82, 87–88
Siegel, Daniel J., 29–30
slavery, 134
sleep, 52–53; chronotypes for, 45–46; health relation to, 47–48
Smarter Balanced assessment, 108
social awareness, 2, 74, 104, 109
social-emotional learning (SEL). *See specific topics*
social-emotional needs, language for, 123
social groups, 94
social intelligence, 74
social media, 6, 49, 106
social teaching practices, culture relation to, 17–18
society, 22, 66, 135; children affected by, 7, 8, 10
socioeconomic status: empathy relation to, 106; of teenagers, 131
socioemotional issues, for children, 3
solutions: in conflict resolution, 91–92; for consequences, 73
"spin the wheel," 74
staff meetings, 108, 109
standardized tests, 67, 102. *See also* assessments
start time, of school, 52–53
STEM programs, 129
stimulus, control of, 51
stories, 82, 87; self-image in, 53
strategies, 42; for relationship building, 115; stress reduction, 41; teaching, 50
stress, 31, 35, 89, 127; in ACE, 90, 95–96; burnout relation to, 43; mindfulness effect on, 131; from perception of future, 7; productivity affected by, 47; sleep affected by, 46; strategies to reduce, 41; support relation to, 105; trauma relation to, 109

stretching, 50
students. *See specific topics*
student-to-student interactions, learning in, 75–76
success, 1, 20–21, 59, 73; grit for, 109; inner worlds relation to, 16–17; leaders relation to, 118, 135; self-management relation to, 42; self-reflection for, 44–45
suicide, 49
superintendent, 118–19
support, 83, 84–85; networks for, 45; stress relation to, 105. *See also* Multi-Tiered Systems of Support; Positive Behavior Interventions and Supports
support staff, for student voices, 133
surveys, 68, 104, 108

tabula rasa (blank slate), 7
tasks, unnecessary: burnout relation to, 20; workloads relation to, 25
teachers. *See specific topics*
teacher shortage, 134
technology: for Khan Academy, 129; negativity relation to, 72
teenagers, socioeconomic status of, 131
tentativeness, 59
Things Fall Apart (book), 34
thoughts, feelings compared to, 20
"3 Sign Practice," of CASEL, 5
time, for support, 83
training, 129–30; for conflict resolution, 127–28; for SEL, 114, 133
transition grades: disciplinary action for, 36; in high school, 4, 32; misbehaviors in, 19
transitions, self-efficacy relation to, 47
trauma, 96; collaboration relation to, 92; conflicts relation to, 95; in early childhood, 105; SEL effect on, 31; stress relation to, 109; of students, 17; trust relation to, 93
trust, 20; in connection, 84; freedom relation to, 9; listening relation

to, 61–62; in relationships, 61, 85; respect relation to, 64; trauma relation to, 93
truth: perception of, 8; self-management relation to, 42
tutoring, 129

underserved populations, wheel of awareness for, 31
understanding, learning relation to, 94
University of Washington, "5 Dimensions of Teaching and Learning" of, 3

values, core, 117
violence, in schools, 6
virtual learning. *See* remote learning
visual learners, 50
voices, of students, 97; for communication, 95; in humanities classes, 130; reflection for, 36; self-awareness relation to, 34; support staff for, 133
vulnerability, 23–24, 36; conflicts affected by, 19; emotions relation to, 43; empathy relation to, 62; respect relation to, 84

warm-up, "spin the wheel" for, 74
well-being, of educators, 15, 89, 117
wellness checks, social-emotional, 3
Western society, blame in, 22
wheel of awareness, 29–30, *30*, 31; emotions determined with, 36
whole-class-directed instruction, lectures compared to, 49
work, distractions effect on, 44
work avoidance, stress relation to, 43
work-life balance, 26
workload, of teachers, 25, 134, 135

Yale Center for Emotional Intelligence, 15

About the Author

Renee G. Carr, EdD, has been working in the field of education since 2007. Dr. Carr has a history of working in international and domestic education and exchange. She is multilingual, speaking Modern Greek, French, and Spanish. Dr. Carr has taught English abroad through the Teaching Assistant Program in France USA. She has worked at American University, nonprofits such as Family Health International (FHI) 360 and the College Board, and Prince George's County and Fairfax County Public Schools, both in the Washington, DC, area. She earned her doctorate in educational administration and policy studies from the George Washington University in May 2019.

The premise of her first book, *Accountability in the Classroom: Using Social-Emotional Learning to Guide School Improvement*, came from her dissertation topic and was published in 2021. She added her own experiences as an educator both from the perspectives of world language education and the COVID-19 crisis. The idea behind her second book, *Kids Before Content: An Educator's Guide on Social-Emotional Learning Competencies*, came from both her dissertation and her experiences with recommending a pilot social-emotional learning program at her school.

www.ingramcontent.com/pod-product-compliance
Lightning Source LLC
Chambersburg PA
CBHW032027230426
43671CB00005B/228